THE ANNOTATED SHAKESPEARE

The Tempest

William Shakespeare

Fully annotated, with an Introduction, by Burton Raffel
With an essay by Harold Bloom

THE ANNOTATED SHAKESPEARE

Yale University Press · New Haven and London

For Richard and Thetis Cusimano, magus et ux

Published with assistance from the Mary Cady Tew Memorial Fund.
Copyright © 2006 by Burton Raffel.

Designed by Rebecca Gibb.
Set in Bembo type by The Composing Room of Michigan, Inc.
Printed in the United States of America by R. R. Donnelley & Sons.

Library of Congress Cataloging-in-Publication Information
Shakespeare, William, 1564–1616.
The Tempest / William Shakespeare ; fully annotated with an introduction
by Burton Raffel ; with an essay by Harold Bloom.
p. cm. — (The annotated Shakespeare)
Includes bibliographical references.
ISBN-13: 978-0-300-10816-3 (pbk.)
ISBN-10: 0-300-10816-8 (pbk.)
1. Fathers and daughters—Drama. 2. Political refugees—Drama.
3. Shipwreck victims—Drama. 4. Magicians—Drama. 5. Islands—
Drama. 6. Spirits—Drama. I. Raffel, Burton. II. Bloom, Harold.
III. Title.
PR2833.A2R34 2006
822.3′3—dc22
2005029102

A catalogue record for this book is available from the British Library.

10 9 8 7 6 5 4 3 2 1

CONTENTS

ABOUT THIS BOOK

In act 2, scene 1, Antonio asks Sebastian a rhetorical question: "Who's the next heir of Naples?" Sebastian replies, "Claribel," this being the king's daughter and, so far as they know, his only surviving child. Antonio then speaks as follows:

Antonio She that is Queen of Tunis. She that dwells
　　Ten leagues beyond man's life. She that from Naples
　　Can have no note, unless the sun were post
　　(The Man i' th' Moon's too slow) till newborn chins
　　Be rough and razorable. She that from whom
　　We all were sea-swallowed, though some cast again,
　　And by that destiny to perform an act
　　Whereof what's past is prologue, what to come
　　In yours, and my, discharge.

This was perfectly understandable, we must assume, to the mostly very average persons who paid to watch Elizabethan plays. But who today can make much sense of it? In this very fully annotated edition, I therefore present this passage, not in the bare form quoted above, but thoroughly supported by bottom-of-the-page notes:

Antonio She that is Queen of Tunis. She that dwells
   Ten leagues beyond man's[1] life. She that from Naples
   Can have no note,[2] unless the sun were post[3]
   (The Man i' th' Moon's too slow[4]) till[5] newborn chins
   Be[6] rough and razorable. She that from whom[7]
   We all were sea-swallowed, though some cast[8] again,
   And by[9] that destiny[10] to perform an act
   Whereof[11] what's past is prologue, what to come
   In yours, and my, discharge.[12]

The modern reader or listener may well better understand this intensely sarcastic speech in context, as the play continues. But without full explanation of words that have over the years shifted in meaning, and usages that have been altered, neither the modern reader nor the modern listener is likely to be equipped for anything like full comprehension.

I believe annotations of this sort create the necessary bridges, from Shakespeare's four-centuries-old English across to ours. Some readers, to be sure, will be able to comprehend unusual, historically different meanings without any glosses. Those not fa-

1. human, civilized
2. written comment
3. the early form of mail was, by horse or coach, from one "post" (for changing horse(s)) to another
4. i.e., the sun takes a single day to complete his circuit; the moon takes 28 days
5. till the time that it takes for
6. to be/become
7. she that from whom=she who away from whom
8. some were cast up
9. because of
10. fact, course of events, predetermined fortune
11. by means of which
12. fulfillment, performance, execution

miliar with the modern meaning of particular words will easily find clear, simple definitions in any modern dictionary. But most readers are not likely to understand Shakespeare's intended meaning, absent such glosses as I here offer.

My annotation practices have followed the same principles used in *The Annotated Milton,* published in 1999, and in my annotated editions of *Hamlet,* published (as the initial volume in this series) in 2003, *Romeo and Juliet* (2004), *Macbeth* (2004), *Othello* (2005), and *The Taming of the Shrew* (2005). Classroom experience has validated these editions. Classes of mixed upper-level undergraduates and graduate students have more quickly and thoroughly transcended language barriers than ever before. This allows the teacher, or a general reader without a teacher, to move more promptly and confidently to the nonlinguistic matters that have made Shakespeare and Milton great and important poets.

It is the inevitable forces of linguistic change, operant in all living tongues, which have inevitably created such wide degrees of obstacles to ready comprehension—not only sharply different meanings, but subtle, partial shifts in meaning that allow us to think we understand when, alas, we do not. Speakers of related languages like Dutch and German also experience this shifting of the linguistic ground. Like early Modern English (ca. 1600) and the Modern English now current, those languages are too close for those who know only one language, and not the other, to be readily able always to recognize what they correctly understand and what they do not. When, for example, a speaker of Dutch says, "Men kofer is kapot," a speaker of German will know that something belonging to the Dutchman is broken ("kapot" = "kaputt" in German, and "men" = "mein"). But without more linguistic awareness than the average person is apt to have, the

German speaker will not identify "kofer" ("trunk" in Dutch) with "Körper"—a modern German word meaning "physique, build, body." The closest word to "kofer" in modern German, indeed, is "Scrankkoffer," which is too large a leap for ready comprehension. Speakers of different Romance languages (French, Spanish, Italian), and all other related but not identical tongues, all experience these difficulties, as well as the difficulty of understanding a text written in their own language five, or six, or seven hundred years earlier. Shakespeare's English is not yet so old that it requires, like many historical texts in French and German, or like Old English texts—for example, *Beowulf*—a modern translation. Much poetry evaporates in translation: language is immensely particular. The sheer *sound* of Dante in thirteenth-century Italian is profoundly worth preserving. So too is the sound of Shakespeare.

I have annotated prosody (metrics) only when it seemed truly necessary or particularly helpful. This play requires much less of such annotation than other volumes in this series. Miranda's opening lines, in act 1, scene 2, are in a sense the start of the play's poetry, most of the first scene being in prose. And Miranda's poetry is supple, flowing, even majestic:

> If by your art, my dearest father, you have
> Put the wild waters in this roar, allay them.
> The sky it seems would pour down stinking pitch,
> But that the sea, mounting to th' welkin's cheek,
> Dashes the fire out.

Not surprisingly, the mellowness of the play seems to have carried over to its metrics.

Readers should have no problem with the silent "e" in past

participles (loved, returned, missed). Except in the few instances where modern usage syllabifies the "e," whenever an "e" in Shakespeare is *not* silent, it is marked "è." The notation used for prosody, which is also used in the explanation of Elizabethan pronunciation, follows the extremely simple form of my *From Stress to Stress: An Autobiography of English Prosody* (see "Further Reading," near the end of this book). Syllables with metrical stress are capitalized; all other syllables are in lowercase letters. I have managed to employ normalized Elizabethan spellings, in most indications of pronunciation, but I have sometimes been obliged to deviate, in the higher interest of being understood.

I have annotated, as well, a limited number of such other matters, sometimes of interpretation, sometimes of general or historical relevance, as have seemed to me seriously worthy of inclusion. These annotations have been most carefully restricted: this is not intended to be a book of literary commentary. It is for that reason that the glossing of metaphors has been severely restricted. There is almost literally no end to discussion and/or analysis of metaphor, especially in Shakespeare. To yield to temptation might well be to double or triple the size of this book—and would also change it from a historically oriented language guide to a work of an unsteadily mixed nature. In the process, I believe, neither language nor literature would be well or clearly served.

Where it seemed useful, and not obstructive of important textual matters, I have modernized spelling, including capitalization. Spelling is not on the whole a basic issue, but punctuation and lineation must be given high respect. The Quarto and the Folio use few exclamation marks or semicolons, which is to be sure a matter of the conventions of a very different era. Still, our modern preferences cannot be lightly substituted for what is, after a fashion, the closest thing to a Shakespeare manuscript we are likely ever to have. We do not know whether these particular seventeenth-century printers, like most of that time, were responsible for question marks, commas, periods and, especially, all-purpose colons, or whether these particular printers tried to follow their handwritten sources. Nor do we know if those sources, or what part thereof, might have been in Shakespeare's own hand. But in spite of these equivocations and uncertainties, it remains true that, to a very considerable extent, punctuation tends to result from just how the mind responsible for that punctuating *hears* the text. And twenty-first-century minds have no business, in such matters, overruling seventeenth-century ones. Whoever the compositors were, they were more or less Shakespeare's contemporaries, and we are not.

Accordingly, when the original printed text uses a comma, we are being signaled that *they* (whoever "they" were) heard the text, not coming to a syntactic stop, but continuing to some later stopping point. To replace commas with editorial periods is thus risky and on the whole an undesirable practice. (Dramatic action, to be sure, may require us, for twenty-first-century readers, to highlight what four-hundred-year-old punctuation standards may not make clear—and may even, at times, misrepresent.)

When the printed text has a colon, what we are being signaled is that *they* heard a syntactic stop—though not necessarily or even usually the particular kind of syntactic stop we associate, today, with the colon. It is therefore inappropriate to substitute editorial commas for original colons. It is also inappropriate to employ editorial colons when *their* syntactic usage of colons does not match ours. In general, the closest thing to *their* syntactic sense of the colon is our (and their) period.

The Folio's interrogation (question) marks, too, merit extremely respectful handling. In particular, editorial exclamation marks should very rarely be substituted for the Folio's interrogation marks.

It follows from these considerations that the movement and sometimes the meaning of what we must take to be Shakespeare's *Tempest* will at times be different, depending on whose punctuation we follow, *theirs* or our own. I have tried, here, to use the printed seventeenth-century text as a guide to both *hearing* and *understanding* what Shakespeare wrote.

Since the original printed texts of (there not being, as there never are for Shakespeare, any surviving manuscripts) are frequently careless as well as self-contradictory, I have been relatively free with the wording of stage directions—and in some cases have added brief directions, to indicate who is speaking to whom. I have made no emendations; I have necessarily been obliged to make choices. Textual decisions have been annotated when the differences between or among the original printed texts seem either marked or of unusual interest.

In the interests of compactness and brevity, I have employed in my annotations (as consistently as I am able) a number of stylistic and typographical devices:

- The annotation of a single word does not repeat that word

- The annotation of more than one word repeats the words being annotated, which are followed by an equals sign and then by the annotation; the footnote number in the text is placed after the last of the words being annotated

- In annotations of a single word, alternative meanings are usually separated by commas; if there are distinctly different ranges of meaning, the annotations are separated by arabic numerals inside parentheses—(1), (2), and so on; in more complexly worded annotations, alternative meanings expressed by a single word are linked by a forward slash, or solidus: /

- Explanations of textual meaning are not in parentheses; comments about textual meaning are

- Except for proper nouns, the word at the beginning of all annotations is in lower case

- Uncertainties are followed by a question mark, set in parentheses: (?)

- When particularly relevant, "translations" into twenty-first-century English have been added, in parentheses

- Annotations of repeated words are *not* repeated. Explanations of the *first* instance of such common words are followed by the sign ★. Readers may easily track down the first annotation, using the brief Finding List at the back of the book. Words with entirely separate meanings are annotated *only* for meanings no longer current in Modern English.

The most important typographical device here employed is the sign ★ placed after the first (and only) annotation of words and phrases occurring more than once. There is an alphabetically arranged listing of such words and phrases in the Finding List at the back of the book. The Finding List contains no annotations but simply gives the words or phrases themselves and the numbers of the relevant act, the scene within that act, and the footnote number within that scene for the word's first occurrence.

INTRODUCTION

First performed, so far as we know, in 1611, and probably written either in that year or in 1610–1611, *The Tempest* is very likely the last play that Shakespeare wrote entirely on his own. *Henry VIII* has been dated from 1612–1613, and *The Two Noble Kinsmen* from 1613, but the latter play was written with John Fletcher, and the former (if it is, as generally conjectured, a collaborative effort) with an undetermined writer or writers. *Cardenio,* 1613, and fairly clearly drawn from Miguel de Cervantes's *Don Quijote,* is known to have been written with Fletcher, but the play has been lost. *The Winter's Tale* is conjecturally dated from 1610–11, just before *The Tempest.*

Whatever the play's exact place in Shakespeare's work, it remains a profoundly autumnal work.

> We are such stuff
> As dreams are made on, and our little life
> Is rounded with a sleep.
>
> (4.1.156–158)

Spoken after the magical wedding pageantry of act 4, and by Prospero, who is the center and narrative fulcrum of the play, the *sense* of these beautiful lines is not unprecedented in Shakespeare's work. But the wistful, retrospectively oriented *tone* is so remarkably plain, all through this brilliantly mellow theater piece, that critics have quite naturally assumed an autobiographical motif. Pushing the age of fifty and just about to retire from a lifetime in and around the London stage, surely Shakespeare wove his own life as a stage "magician" into this tale of a perhaps fifty-year-old real-life magician, about to retire from the magical island ("stage"?) where for a dozen years he has ruled? But there is not a bit of supporting evidence. Autobiographical speculation fits, and it is appealing; whether it is true we do not know.

The structure and narrative balance of *The Tempest* fits, to some extent, with that of other late and more or less ruminative Shakespeare plays. In the matter of approximate stage time (*not* lines spoken) allotted to particular characters, *The Tempest* assigns the major amount of active presence to Prospero, roughly 52 percent. That is close to the figure received by King Lear, in the play bearing his name. The downward spread in approximate stage time, in *Lear* (1605–1606), runs from the second most often heard-from character, Kent, who receives 39 percent, to 17 percent for Albany and Cornwall; this embraces nine characters. And the downward spread of assigned stage-time in *The Tempest* also embraces nine characters, as follows:

Ariel, 31 percent
Sebastian, 28 percent
Alonso, 28 percent
Miranda, 27 percent
Caliban, 25 percent
Gonzalo, 24 percent

Antonio, 22 percent
Stephano 21 percent
Ferdinand, 17 percent
Trinculo, 17 percent.

And in *Measure for Measure* (1604), there is a somewhat similar balance, including, however, a total of only five characters, and running from 44 percent for both Isabella and the Duke, down to 17 percent for Pompey. The more ruminative of Shakespeare's seventeenth-century plays certainly employ varying stage-time distributions. In *Hamlet* (1600–1601) stage time varies from a totally dominate 66 percent for Hamlet to 17 percent for Ophelia, with five other characters in between these high and low figures. Stage-time figures in *Othello* (1603–1604) show Iago at 64 percent, Othello at 59 percent, followed thereafter by four other characters whose stage-time runs from 32 percent (Emilia, Iago's wife), to 17 percent for Roderigo, Iago's much-abused victim.

But *Lear, Hamlet,* and *Othello* are unmistakably tragedies; *Measure for Measure* is an exceedingly strange comedy—and what is *The Tempest?* Fitting *The Tempest* into the three highly approximate genre descriptions in traditional use—comedies, tragedies, and history plays—is no simpler a task than trying to categorize the play's structure. It is clearly neither a tragedy nor a history. But is it truly a comedy? Shakespeare's former colleagues, when in 1623 they published the First Folio, not only gave *The Tempest* pride of place, putting it smack in the front of the book, but definitely labeled it comedic. And it does have significant comedic pages, as it also has two characters—Stephano and Trinculo—who are without question outright clowns. But *Hamlet* too gives about 20 percent of its length to comedy of one sort or another, as does *Lear* and also an earlier tragedy, *Romeo and Juliet*. Is *The Tempest* a romance, as some have suggested? Is it in some ways more like, say, *Midsummer Night's Dream* or even *Twelfth Night?* These latter are both "comedies" and yet resonate with large elements of that something-more, that something-different, and yes, that something-unclassifiable which is part and parcel of what distinguishes Shakespeare from all other dramatists, whether in his own time and or any other, and whether in his own language and culture or any other.

The Tempest is a ripe, wise play, and a meditatively sad play, and a funny play, and a majestically grand play. And more, for Shakespeare's tough, probing intelligence, even as it never for a moment leaves the fictive world it so vividly creates, pushes into realms both as distinct and as eternally unsettled as the comparative virtues of civilization and nature; the dynamics of social order and hierarchies; relationships between peoples (and beings?) of different origin; the variable realities of loyalty, love, and magic; and the role of the divine in human existence. Neither Shakespeare nor anyone else has final answers to any of these matters. But Shakespeare's wise autumnal explorations, and the gorgeous writing with which he prosecutes them, make *The Tempest* worthy of virtually endless investigation.

Item: Caliban. We have only a sometimes vague account of his origins, but there can be no doubt as to the opinions and beliefs of the Folio's editors. Caliban is there described, in the list of characters printed after the text of the play, as "a savage and deformed slave." "Savage" had a number of meanings, in Shakespeare's time, "wild, undomesticated, uncivilized, rude, ungovernable, ferocious," all of them (except perhaps the full sense of "ferocious") applicable to Caliban. A "slave" was someone in the full control of someone else; the word carried additional and negative senses of contempt and disapproval ("rascal"), as well as that of a submissive or devoted servant, in which latter sense Shakespeare uses it in the first scene of the first act of *The Taming of the Shrew*, 1593–1594). But the third element of the Folio description, "deformed," meaning "misshapen, shapeless, monstrous, ugly," is arguably the most important, for it helps in defining Caliban's genetic being. Caliban's mother, Sycorax, was a witch, exiled from her native Algeria to the island of the play, where she arrived, pregnant with Caliban, and where he was born and has grown up. We do not know for sure who or what was Caliban's father, though Prospero in a moment of anger says that Caliban was "got [engendered] by the Devil himself" and we know it was widely believed that witches copulated with devils. Prospero also says Caliban "was not honored with a human shape"; Alonso, on seeing the monster for the first time, declares, "This is a strange thing as e'er I looked on"; Trinculo is never clear whether Caliban is "a man or a fish"; and Antonio, admittedly sneeringly, also calls Caliban a "plain fish." But Shakespeare was not as concerned with Caliban's origins and physical/genetic (or, again, "racial"?) nature as with his character and actions; we will never have certainty on these matters.

What *is* certain is that, though Caliban is perceived as a "monster," he often speaks with the tongue of an angel:

I prithee let me bring thee where crabs grow,
And I with my long nails will dig thee pig-nuts,
Show thee a jay's nest, and instruct thee how
To snare the nimble marmozet. I'll bring thee

To clust'ring filberts, and sometimes I'll get thee
Young scamels from the rock. Wilt thou go with me?

(2.2.156—161)

This delicate and delightful invitation may be wasted on a pair of
drunken sots like Stephano and Trinculo. It remains the passion-
ate invocation of a country-bred man's boyhood pleasures, distinctly comparable to those of Mark Twain in *Huckleberry Finn*.
And when Stephano and Trinculo, obviously city-bred (or at least
city-broken), are frightened by the nighttime sounds of the island, Caliban speaks to them even more enchantingly:

Be not afeard, the isle is full of noises,
Sounds, and sweet airs, that give delight and hurt not.
Sometimes a thousand twangling instruments
Will hum about mine ears, and sometimes voices,
That if I then had waked after long sleep,
Will make me sleep again, and then in dreaming
The clouds methought would open, and show riches
Ready to drop upon me, that when I waked
I cried to dream again.

(3.2.131—139)

There is sadness in these evocations, and others like them. This is,
as I have said, an autumnally wistful play. But it cannot be accidental that Shakespeare consistently gives lines of such loveliness
to a "savage and deformed slave," as it cannot be accidental that,
while other "low" characters in the play speak in prose, Caliban is
regularly poetic. He can be lecherously ugly, he is usually cow-
ardly, and his social and moral perspectives are indeed "savage."
But the tenderness we often hear from his mouth seems pretty
clearly a mark (even if qualified) of Shakespeare's favor.

Which is why it makes no great sense, judged against the actual text of the play, to argue that Caliban is "right" and Prospero "wrong," the one cast as an exploited colonial and the other as an exploitative colonizer, an imperialist. When Caliban, who had been languageless, first encounters Prospero, the dead witch's son is taught to use language. Now he rejects the gift.

> You taught me language, and my profit on't
> Is, I know how to curse. The red plague rid you
> For learning me your language!
>
> (1.2.364–366)

What Stephen J. Greenblatt sees in this rejection is its "devastating justness. Ugly, rude, savage, Caliban nevertheless achieves for an instant an absolute if intolerably bitter moral victory . . . a momentary victory that is, quite simply, an assertion of inconsolable human pain and bitterness."[1] Eric Cheyfitz, who brings in a great deal of anticolonialistic rhetoric to support Greenblatt's approach, goes still further. Using Caliban's name is "an imperial and colonial act of translation. . . . [It is] an utterance in the colonial / imperialist process . . . that I am describing and that, I will argue, the play itself describes."[2] Yet merely saying that an argument is "quite simply" correct does not make it either simple or correct. Prospero is neither a colonizer nor an imperialist. He does not choose to land on the island but, rather, saves his and his young daughter's lives, after they have been abandoned to die at sea, by coming ashore anywhere he can. Until Caliban tries to rape his daughter, Prospero is reasonably gracious and kind. It is not hard to understand Caliban's discomfiture, having lost control of the island to the only humans, other than his mother, he has ever seen. It is not hard to understand his psychological state. However, to extrapolate comprehension of simplistic wrath into a highly moral deed, and then to further extrapolate that "morality" into a sweeping condemnation and a singularly far-fetched reading of *The Tempest* as a whole, is, quite simply indeed, defective thinking.

Item: Ariel. Until the time at which the play opens, this creature of the air, a sprite of nonhuman origin and many supernatural powers, has been one of the small number of personages (four in all) present on the island. He has unequivocally charmed and fascinated audiences and commentators for four hundred years. We know almost nothing of Ariel's background, other than that he served the witch Sycorax and was punished by her for his unwillingness to do something unsavory. Though not human, he plainly lives by a moral code, as the following brief dialogue about the guilty humans enchanted by Prospero demonstrates:

Ariel   Your charm so strongly works 'em
    That if you now beheld them, your affections
    Would become tender.
Prospero   Dost thou think so, spirit?
Ariel   Mine would, sir, were I human.
Prospero   And mine shall.
    Hast thou (which art but air) a touch, a feeling
    Of their afflictions, and shall not myself,
    One of their kind, that relish all as sharply,
    Passion as they, be kindlier moved than thou art?

                                        (5.1.17–24)

The play's other nonhuman, Caliban, can speak most appealingly, but Ariel can speak nobly—and effectively, as immature/unripened Caliban cannot. Prospero is won to forgiveness, after this appeal.

But it is Ariel's disengagement from humanity, rather than his ability to empathize with and address himself to human emotions, that most attracts us. When we first meet Ariel, as Prospero in act 1, scene 2 summons the sprite to appear to him, Ariel explains that

> I come
> To answer thy best pleasure, be't to fly,
> To swim, to dive into the fire, to ride
> On the curlèd clouds. To thy strong bidding task
> Ariel and all his quality.
>
> (1.2.189–193)

Humans have always envied birds their ability to freely leave the surface of the earth and to fly where they will. Ariel can do this, and much more. Obviously he can speak, and he can sing and play voiceless "solemn music"; he can fly infinitely faster than birds; he can be visible or invisible, as he chooses; he can transform himself into and seem fully to be all sorts of creatures, from demigoddesses and fearsome harpies to drummer boys.

His relationship with Prospero has been seen in a good many different lights. Ariel's basic and clearly dominant motive is the gaining (or regaining?) of his freedom, which Prospero has promised he will have, but only after a pledge of service has been fully honored. Ariel grows restive, Prospero threatens:

> If thou more murmur'st, I will rend an oak
> And peg thee in his knotty entrails till
> Thou hast howled away twelve winters.
>
> (1.2.295–297)

But the moment Ariel begs his master's pardon, and promises gracious compliance, Prospero completely changes his tone:

Ariel Pardon, master.
   I will be correspondent to command
   And do my spriting, gently.
Prospero   Do so. And after two days
   I will discharge thee.

(1.2.297–300)

At which, Ariel fairly leaps up and down with joy:

   That's my noble master!
   What shall I do? Say what? What shall I do?

(1.2.300–301)

Nor is the sense that seems to emerge, here, of a genuine emotional link between these two totally unlike characters, in any way a mere will-o-the-wisp. Prospero's delight in Ariel's actions, many times expressed, is matched by Ariel's desire both to please and to be praised. In act 4, scene 1 we have the following exchange:

Ariel   Before you can say "Come," and "Go,"
   And breathe twice, and cry "So, so,"
   Each one, tripping on his toe,
   Will be here with mop and mow.
   Do you love me, master? No?
Prospero Dearly, my delicate Ariel.

(4.1.44–49)

Prospero's praise for his sprite grows warmer, as the play progresses. When in act 1, scene 2 Ariel, following instructions, goes off to transform himself into a water nymph, Prospero says: "Fine apparition. My quaint Ariel, / Hark in thine ear." After Ariel's thunderous representation of a harpy, in act 3, scene 3, Prospero becomes more loquacious: "Bravely the figure of this harpy hast thou / Performed, my Ariel. A grace it had, devouring. / Of my instruction hast thou nothing bated / In what thou hadst to say." Later in act 4, Prospero becomes distinctly affectionate, using pet, affectionate language: "This was well done, my bird" By act 5, the declaration of affection becomes completely explicit: "Why that's my dainty Ariel. I shall miss thee, / But yet thou shalt have freedom." And Ariel over and over replies to Prospero with the most compelling of ebullient gracefulness, saying at the end of act 1, "To th' syllable," and in the first scene of act 5, "I drink the air before me, and return / Or ere your pulse twice beat." But it is Ariel's freedom song, coming just before this last-cited, bubbling declaration, that best expresses the character's fullest nature:

> Where the bee sucks, there suck I,
> In a cowslip's bell I lie,
> There I couch when owls do cry,
> On the bat's back I do fly
>   after summer merrily.
> Merrily, merrily, shall I live now
> Under the blossom that hangs on the bough.

(5.1.88–94)

Shakespeare's plays ring with song, but this may well be the most plangently affecting of all. How can one *not* love Ariel?

Item: Prospero. Autobiographical or not, Prospero remains—like his creator—both complex and, ultimately, baffling. Did his first audience, essentially the court of King James, think that Prospero had been a *good* ruler, in his first years as Duke of Milan? For some of them, surely, it would have been enough that he had been a ruler, a legitimate, consecrated ruler. But others were likely to have seen a significant inconsistency between Prospero's *rights* and his *obligations*. No one expected a ruler to be angelically good; rulers were plainly human beings. But some degree of balance was expected, and Prospero had none. Obsessed with magical art, he spent all of his time with his books and absolutely none in his role as ruler. That is, he wanted what he wanted and completely disregarded what he *owed*. His all-powerful delegate was of course his brother, and if his own brother could not be trusted, who could? But humanistic expectations were realistic and went beyond mere trust. The Duke in *Measure for Measure* is rather similarly not in complete balance, but he is sufficiently self-aware that he spends the length of the play checking both on himself and on his trusted delegate. Prospero, at least in his earlier years, was beyond such basic, arguably elementary caution.

It is not, then, that Prospero was a bad duke, but that he was in effect a demi-duke. He had but did not use his powers, for either good or evil; he indulged himself in his wealth and leisure; he returned nothing, so far as we are told, to anyone, either below or cognate with him. It has been suggested that he probably ignored his wife and even his young daughter. But we do not know anything about these matters. Shakespeare does perhaps indicate, though very left-handedly at best, that Prospero was not an ideal husband. Why else, we may wonder, would he omit to tell Miranda anything whatever about her mother? Not to mention the duchess's name is understandable: she would have been known, even to her husband and certainly to her daughter, by one or another respectful title. But to virtually ignore her existence may—may—be some indication of something about which we do not know enough to pass judgment. However, the duke's human imbalance, in his earlier years, is most clearly presented.

The setting for his return to balance—totally unlike well-populated and cosmopolitan Milan—is an unnamed island somewhere in the Mediterranean Sea. And *place* is basic to humanistic notions of balance. That quintessential humanist, Erasmus of Rotterdam, describes the fundamental basis of "peace" in glowingly place-oriented terms: "Yet even members of the vegetable world, trees and herbs, show an attraction toward others of the same species. Vines embrace elms, peaches welcome the encirclement of vines. The world of the insensible appreciates the benefits of peace."[3] Johan Huizinga emphasizes that such ideas were in no way unique to Erasmus: "The whole Renaissance cherished that wish of reposeful, blithe, and yet serious intercourse of good and wise friends in the cool shade of a house under trees, where serenity and harmony would dwell. The age yearned for the realization of simplicity, sincerity, truth and nature. . . . In Erasmus's writings that ideal wish ever recurs in the shape of a friendly walk, followed by a meal in a garden-house."[4] And Rosalie L. Colie evokes wonderfully well how these perspectives underlie the very real, inherent magic of *The Tempest*'s island: "In the case of this uncharted island, its associations with the 'still-vexed Bermoothes' and with Mediterranean islands like Corfu only serve to make its locale more mysterious, its magic qualities truly leagues beyond ordinary life. The island is far from simple: in the midst of its strange, transubstantiating perfections, Caliban is after all at home. . . . The island can nourish both the natural and the supernatural in man, but it must be well-ruled, well-regulated, to become the gracious state that it is in *The Tempest*. Shielded as it is from cartography and from history, the island suggests ideals for human behavior rather than imposes them."[5] Or as Harold C. Goddard puts it, "Of the many universal symbols on which *The Tempest* is erected that of the island is fundamental. An island is a bit of a higher element rising out of a lower."[6]

Twelve years on the island guarantees Prospero nothing. He appears to have perfected his magical powers, though we are not told how potent they had already become, in Milan. He has plainly not perfected himself. As I have noted, the final and, for a Christian, the basic reformatory act of forgiveness is directly owing to the nonhuman intervention of Ariel. Many commentators have noted, and some have been baffled by, what seem to be contradictions in Prospero's attitudes and actions. He appears harsh and punitive, then seems to turn around and rather abruptly decide to be gentle and kind. Yet these are no more contradictory than the idea of a ruler who does not rule. Prospero is not so much indecisive as, like all human beings, unfinished. Again, it is not at all that he is a bad man but that he like everyone else is inescapably flawed. It has often been said, in the fifty years since full knowledge of the Holocaust was spread across the world, that "there is a Nazi in every one of us." Prospero does not seem a likely candidate for Nazihood—but what of Antonio, the now-deposed deposer? And what of Sebastian, the would-be king who was quite prepared to murder his brother?

There are no plain answers. "There is, then, an irresistible tendency to expand this play," remarked Muriel Bradbrook.[7] There is indeed. And the continuing wonder is that the play simultaneously evokes, justifies, and provides sustenance for such expansions. It is very nearly the shortest in the entire canon of Shakespeare's stage work, but it is by no means the easiest to encompass, let alone be done with. As Charles Lamb declared, almost two hundred years ago, "I cannot help being of opinion that the plays of Shakespeare are less calculated for performance on a stage, than those of almost any other dramatist whatever. Their distinguishing excellence is a reason that they should be so. There is so much in them, which comes not under the province of acting, with which eye, and tone, and gesture, have nothing to do." [8] Lamb may not have been 100 percent right, but who are we to say he was wrong?

Notes

1. Stephen J. Greenblatt, *Learning to Curse: Essays in Early Modern Culture* (New York: Routledge, 1990), 25–26.
2. Eric Cheyfitz, *The Poetics of Imperialism: Translation and Colonization from The Tempest to Tarzan* (New York: Oxford University Press, 1991), 41, 61.
3. Erasmus, "The Complaint of Peace," in John P. Dolan, ed., *The Essential Erasmus* (New York: New American Library, 1964), 178.
4. Johan Huizinga, *Erasmus and the Age of Reformation* (New York: Harper and Row, 1957), 104.
5. Rosalie L. Colie, *Shakespeare's Living Art* (Princeton, N.J.: Princeton University Press, 1974), 299.
6. Harold C. Goddard, *The Meaning of Shakespeare*, 2 vols. (Chicago: University of Chicago Press, 1951), 2:287.
7. M. C. Bradbrook, *Shakespeare: The Poet in His World* (New York: Columbia University Press, 1978), 234.
8. Charles Lamb, *The Complete Works and Letters* (New York: Modern Library, 1935), 291–292.

SOME ESSENTIALS OF THE
SHAKESPEAREAN STAGE

The Stage

- There was no *scenery* (backdrops, flats, and so on).

- Compared to today's elaborate, high-tech productions, the
  Elizabethan stage had few *on-stage* props. These were mostly
  handheld: a sword or dagger, a torch or candle, a cup or flask.
  Larger props, such as furniture, were used sparingly.

- Costumes (some of which were upper-class castoffs,
  belonging to the individual actors) were elaborate. As in most
  premodern and very hierarchical societies, clothing was the
  distinctive mark of who and what a person was.

- What the actors *spoke,* accordingly, contained both the
  dramatic and narrative material we have come to expect in a
  theater (or movie house) and (1) the setting, including details
  of the time of day, the weather, and so on, and (2) the
  occasion. The *dramaturgy* is thus very different from that of
  our own time, requiring much more attention to verbal and
  gestural matters. Strict realism was neither intended nor, under
  the circumstances, possible.

- There was *no curtain*. Actors entered and left via doors in the back of the stage, behind which was the "tiring-room," where actors put on or changed their costumes.
- In *public theaters* (which were open-air structures), there was no *lighting;* performances could take place only in daylight hours.
- For *private* theaters, located in large halls of aristocratic houses, candlelight illumination was possible.

The Actors

- Actors worked in *professional,* for-profit companies, sometimes organized and owned by other actors, and sometimes by entrepreneurs who could afford to erect or rent the company's building. Public theaters could hold, on average, two thousand playgoers, most of whom viewed and listened while standing. Significant profits could be and were made. Private theaters were smaller, more exclusive.
- There was *no director.* A book-holder/prompter/props manager, standing in the tiring-room behind the backstage doors, worked from a text marked with entrances and exits and notations of any special effects required for that particular script. A few such books have survived. Actors had texts only of their own parts, speeches being cued to a few prior words. There were few and often no rehearsals, in our modern use of the term, though there was often some coaching of individuals. Since Shakespeare's England was largely an oral culture, actors learned their parts rapidly and retained them for years. This was *repertory* theater, repeating popular plays and introducing some new ones each season.

- *Women* were not permitted on the professional stage. Most female roles were acted by *boys;* elderly women were played by grown men.

The Audience

- London's professional theater operated in what might be called a "red-light" district, featuring brothels, restaurants, and the kind of *open-air entertainment* then most popular, like bear-baiting (in which a bear, tied to a stake, was set on by dogs).

- A theater audience, like most of the population of Shakespeare's England, was largely made up of *illiterates.* Being able to read and write, however, had nothing to do with intelligence or concern with language, narrative, and characterization. People attracted to the theater tended to be both extremely verbal and extremely volatile. Actors were sometimes attacked, when the audience was dissatisfied; quarrels and fights were relatively common. Women were regularly in attendance, though no reliable statistics exist.

- Drama did not have the cultural esteem it has in our time, and plays were not regularly printed. Shakespeare's often appeared in book form, but not with any supervision or other involvement on his part. He wrote a good deal of nondramatic poetry as well, yet so far as we know he did not authorize or supervise *any* work of his that appeared in print during his lifetime.

- Playgoers, who had paid good money to see and hear, plainly gave dramatic performances careful, detailed attention. For some closer examination of such matters, see Burton Raffel, "Who Heard the Rhymes and How: Shakespeare's Dramaturgical Signals," *Oral Tradition* 11 (October 1996): 190–221, and Raffel, "Metrical Dramaturgy in Shakespeare's Earlier Plays," *CEA Critic* 57 (Spring–Summer 1995): 51–65.

The Tempest

CHARACTERS (DRAMATIS PERSONAE)

Alonso (King of Naples)

Sebastian (Alonso's brother)

Ferdinand (Alonso's son)

Prospero (true[1] Duke of Milan)

Antonio (Prospero's brother, usurping[2] Duke of Milan)

Gonzalo (an honest old counselor)

Adrian (a lord)

Francisco (a lord)

Caliban (a savage and deformed slave)

Trinculo (a jester)

Stephano (a drunken butler)[3]

Master[4] *of a ship*

Boatswain[5]

Mariners[6]

Miranda (Prospero's daughter)

Ariel (an airy Spirit)

Iris, Ceres, Juno, nymphs, reapers (Spirits), *and other Spirits attending on Prospero*

1 real, legitimate
2 illegally taking over as
3 in charge of the wine cellar and of serving wine★
4 captain
5 ship's officer (BOZin)
6 sailors

Act I

SCENE I

A ship at sea

TEMPESTUOUS NOISE OF THUNDER AND LIGHTNING

ENTER MASTER AND BOATSWAIN

Master   Boatswain!

Boatswain Here, master. What cheer?[1]

Master   Good.[2] Speak to the mariners. Fall to't,[3] yarely,[4] or
we run ourselves aground. Bestir,[5] bestir.

EXIT MASTER

ENTER MARINERS

Boatswain Heigh,[6] my hearts,[7] cheerly,[8] cheerly, my hearts!   5

1 what cheer = how goes it?
2 (1) good man/fellow, (2) I'm glad you're here
3 fall to't = get working at it
4 promptly/diligently (YAreLEE)
5 get busy, exert yourselves
6 exclamation of encouragement
7 hearties, comrades
8 with a will, lively, heartily

Yare,[9] yare! Take in[10] the topsail.[11] Tend[12] to th' master's
whistle. (*to the storm*) Blow till thou burst thy wind, if room
enough.[13]

ENTER ALONSO, SEBASTIAN, ANTONIO, FERDINAND,
GONZALO, AND OTHERS

Alonso   Good boatswain, have care. Where's the master? Play
10   the men.[14]

Boatswain I pray[15] now, keep[16] below.

Antonio   Where is the master, boson?

Boatswain Do you not hear him? You mar[17] our labor,[18] keep[19]
your cabins. You do[20] assist the storm.

15 *Gonzalo*   Nay, good[21] be patient.

Boatswain When the séa is. Hence,[22] what cares[23] these
roarers[24] for the name of king? To cabin, silence! Trouble
us not.

Gonzalo   Good, yet remember whom thou hast aboard.

---

9 at once, right now
10 furl, roll up
11 (TOPsil)
12 listen
13 if room enough = just as long as we have sufficient space between ship and
shore
14 act/work like men (to boatswain? or to all the sailors?)
15 pray/request★ you
16 stay, remain
17 (1) hamper, interrupt, (2) spoil, ruin★
18 work, exertion★
19 keep to
20 you do = you really/very much ("do" is used as an intensifier)
21 good man/fellow
22 leave, go away
23 (word forms and syntax do not always follow the rules of modern English)
24 roaring waves/winds (also used to describe bullies/drunks)

Boatswain None that I more love than myself. You are a   20
   counselor. If you can command these elements to silence, and
   work[25] the peace of the present,[26] we will not hand[27] a rope
   more, use your authority. If you cannot, give thanks you have
   lived so long, and make yourself ready in your cabin for the
   mischance of the hour,[28] if it so hap.[29] (*to sailors*) Cheerly,   25
   good hearts! (*to passengers*) Out of our way, I say.

EXIT BOATSWAIN

Gonzalo I have[30] great comfort from this fellow. Methinks[31]
   he hath no drowning mark[32] upon him, his complexion[33] is
   perfect gallows.[34] Stand fast,[35] good Fate, to his hanging,
   make the rope of his destiny our cable,[36] for our own doth[37]   30
   little advantage.[38] If he be not born to be hanged, our case[39]
   is miserable.

EXEUNT[40] PASSENGERS

25 accomplish, produce
26 the present = the present occasion/affair in hand
27 touch, handle
28 mischance of the hour = disaster/calamity* of the present moment
29 come about (the noun "hap" = luck, chance, fortune)*
30 get, receive
31 it seems to me*
32 sign (physical features were regarded as predictive)
33 look, appearance
34 proverbial: those meant to die by hanging are never drowned
35 stand fast = remain unshaken
36 thick, strong rope used to anchor ships
37 gives, causes, brings (doth = do-eth)
38 benefit
39 state, situation*
40 plural form of exit: "they exit"

ENTER BOATSWAIN

Boatswain Down with the topmast![41] Yare, lower, lower, bring
her to try wi' th' maincourse.[42]

A CRY WITHIN[43]

35 A plague upon this howling! They[44] are louder than the
weather or our office.[45]

ENTER SEBASTIAN, ANTONIO, AND GONZALO

Yet again? What do you here? Shall we give o'er[46] and
drown? Have you a mind to sink?

Sebastian A pox o' your throat, you bawling, blasphemous,
40 incharitable dog!

Boatswain Work you then.

Antonio Hang cur, hang, you whoreson,[47] insolent
noisemaker, we are less afraid to be drowned than thou art.

Gonzalo I'll warrant[48] him for[49] drowning, though the ship
45 were no stronger than a nutshell, and as leaky as an
unstanched[50] wench.

Boatswain Lay her ahold,[51] ahold, set her two courses[52] off to

---

41 topmast: an extension, bound onto the mainmast, and detachable when
   necessary to reduce wind pressure on the ship
42 to try wi' th' maincourse = to separate from the mainsail
43 offstage
44 the passengers
45 jobs, activities, functioning ("work")★
46 give o'er = give up
47 son of a whore, bastard
48 guarantee, promise, assure★
49 in the case of ("against")
50 (1) unsatisfied, unsated, *or* (2) insufficiently padded during menstruation
51 lay her ahold = bring the ship closer to the wind (all ships being female)
52 points on the compass

sea again, lay her off.[53]

Mariners   All lost,[54] to prayers, to prayers, all lost!

EXEUNT

Boatswain What, must our mouths be cold?[55]   50
Gonzalo   The King and Prince at prayers, let's[56] assist them,
For our case is as theirs.
Sebastian   I'am[57] out of patience.
Antonio   We are merely[58] cheated of our lives by drunkards.
This wide-chapped[59] rascal – (*to Boatswain*) Would thou
might'st lie drowning
The washing of ten tides![60]
Gonzalo   He'll be hanged yet,   55
Though every drop of water swear against it,
And gape at wid'st to glut him.[61]

CONFUSED NOISE WITHIN

Mercy on us!
We split, we split!
Farewell, my wife and children!   60

---

53 away from the land
54 ruined, destroyed, hopeless
55 cold in the mouth = dead
56 let us
57 I'm
58 absolutely
59 big-mouthed (chap = jaw)★
60 (by law, pirates were to be hanged and left at the low-tide mark until three
    tides had washed over their bodies)
61 gape at wid'st to glut him = open★ at its widest to swallow/gulp him down

Farewell, brother![62]

We split, we split, we split!

Antonio   Let's all sink wi' the King.

Sebastian   Let's take leave of him.

EXIT ANTONIO AND SEBASTIAN

Gonzalo   Now would I give a thousand furlongs[63] of sea for an
65   acre of barren ground. Long heath,[64] brown furze,[65]
anything. The wills above[66] be done, but I would fain[67] die a
dry death.

EXIT GONZALO

---

62 (1) fellow countryman, (2) comrade, friend
63 furlong = one-eighth of a mile
64 tall heather
65 spiny evergreen shrub ("gorse"), brown because dead or dying
66 (see the Paternoster/Lord's Prayer: "Thy will be done")
67 be delighted/rejoice/glad to

SCENE 2

The Island

<small>ENTER PROSPERO AND MIRANDA</small>

Miranda If by your art,[1] my dearest father, you have
    Put the wild waters in this roar,[2] allay[3] them.
    The sky it seems would[4] pour down stinking pitch,[5]
    But that the sea, mounting to th' welkin's cheek,[6]
    Dashes the fire out. O! I have suffered   5
    With those that I saw suffer. A brave[7] vessel,
    Who had, no doubt, some noble creatures in her,
    Dashed all to pieces. O the cry did knock
    Against my very[8] heart. Poor souls, they perished.
    Had I been any god of power, I would   10
    Have sunk the sea within the earth, or e'er[9]
    It should the good ship so have swallowed and
    The fraughting souls[10] within her.
Prospero   Be collected,[11]
    No more amazement.[12] Tell your piteous[13] heart

1 knowledge, learning, skill★
2 tumult, disturbance
3 quell, put down, abate★
4 wants/wishes to (volition was still included in "will"; tenses are not always
  used as in modern English)
5 black tar-like substance★
6 welkin's cheek = the heavens'/sky's face★
7 fine, handsome, worthy★
8 an intensive, here without additional meaning of its own
9 or e'er = before
10 fraughting souls = people being carried
11 composed, self-possessed
12 bewilderment, distraction★ (though lineated as two lines, prosodically –
  metrically – this and the line before it are regarded as a single iambic
  pentameter line: the FRAUGHTing SOULS withIN her BE colLECTed)
13 full of pity/compassion

There's no harm done.

Miranda   O woe the day!

15 Prospero   No harm.

    I have done nothing but[14] in care of[15] thee,

    Of thee my dear one, thee my daughter, who

    Art ignorant of what[16] thou art, nought knowing

    Of whence I am,[17] nor that I am more better

20   Than Prospero, master[18] of a full[19] poor cell,[20]

    And thy no greater[21] father.

Miranda   More to know

    Did never meddle with[22] my thoughts.

Prospero   'Tis time

    I should inform thee farther. Lend thy hand,

    And pluck my magic garment from me.

HE LAYS DOWN HIS MANTLE[23]

                             So,

25   Lie there my art. (to Miranda) Wipe thou thine eyes, have
    comfort.

    The direful[24] spectacle of the wrack[25] which touched

    The very virtue[26] of compassion in thee,

14 except
15 anxiety / responsibility for, attention to, oversight of
16 who (name, station in life)
17 of whence I am = from where I came (and belong)
18 controlling, having authority over
19 entirely, completely, perfectly★
20 dwelling, den
21 no greater = no more highly placed / distinguished
22 meddle with = concern
23 cloak
24 terrible, dreadful
25 shipwreck★
26 very virtue = true / actual / exact★ quality of moral excellence

I have with such provision[27] in mine art
So safely ordered[28] that there is no soul —
No, not so much perdition[29] as an hair —   30
Betid[30] to any creature in the vessel
Which thou heard'st cry, which thou saw'st sink. Sit down,
For thou must now know farther.
Miranda   You have often
Begun to tell me what I am, but stopped
And left me to a bootless inquisition,[31]   35
Concluding, "Stay,[32] not yet."
Prospero   The hour's now come,
The very minute bids thee ope thine ear.
Obey, and be attentive. Canst thou remember
A time before we came unto this cell?
I do not think thou canst, for then thou wast not   40
Out[33] three years old.
Miranda   Certainly sir, I can.
Prospero By what? By any other house, or person?
Of any thing the image, tell me, that
Hath kept with[34] thy remembrance.
Miranda   'Tis far off,
And rather like a dream than an assurance[35]   45
That my remembrance warrants. Had I not

27 foresight, advance preparation
28 regulated, controlled, arranged★
29 destruction, loss, ruin★
30 befallen, happened
31 bootless inquisition = helpless/useless inquiry, search, investigation
32 wait
33 yet, quite
34 kept with = been preserved/saved in
35 certainty

    Four, or five women once, that tended[36] me?

Prospero Thou hadst, and more, Miranda. But how is it

    That this lives in thy mind? What seest thou else[37]

50   In the dark backward and abysm[38] of time?

    If thou rememb'rest aught ere[39] thou cam'st here,

    How thou cam'st here thou mayst.[40]

Miranda   But that I do not.

Prospero Twelve year since, Miranda, twelve year since,

    Thy father was the Duke of Milan[41] and

    A prince[42] of power.

55 *Miranda*   Sir, are not you my father?

Prospero Thy mother was a piece[43] of virtue, and

    She said thou wast my daughter. And thy father

    Was Duke of Milan, and[44] his only heir

    And princess, no worse issued.[45]

Miranda   O the heavens,

60   What foul play[46] had we, that we came from thence?

    Or blessèd[47] was't we did?

Prospero   Both, both, my girl,[48]

    By foul play (as thou say'st) were we heaved[49] thence,

---

36 looked after, attended
37 (1) in addition, (2) otherwise*
38 backward and abysm = back places and bottomless gulf
39 before*
40 may also recall
41 MYlan
42 ruler, sovereign
43 true specimen/picture
44 and you
45 no worse issued = are of no lower importance/standing ("birth")
46 foul play = treacherous dealing/actions
47 good fortune, joyful
48 both BOTH my GIRL
49 carried off, thrown, cast

But blessedly holp[50] hither.

Miranda   O my heart bleeds
  To think o' th' teen[51] that I have turned you to,[52]
  Which is from[53] my remembrance. Please you, farther.[54]   65

Prospero My brother and thy uncle, called Antonio –
  I pray thee, mark[55] me – that a brother should
  Be so perfidious![56] – he, whom next thyself
  Of all the world I loved, and to him put[57]
  The manage of my state,[58] as at that time   70
  Through all the signories[59] it was the first,
  And Prospero the prime[60] duke, being so reputed
  In dignity,[61] and for the liberal arts,[62]
  Without a parallel, those being all[63] my study,
  The government[64] I cast[65] upon my brother,   75
  And to my state grew stranger,[66] being transported[67]
  And rapt[68] in secret[69] studies. Thy false uncle –

50 helped
51 trouble, suffering, grief
52 to think about / remember / go back to
53 gone / absent / lost from
54 go further, continue
55 give your attention to★
56 treacherous, faithless
57 to him put = in him placed
58 Milan was a sovereign city state, like Venice
59 governing bodies
60 principal, first ("number one")
61 honor, excellence, worth
62 liberal arts = arts and sciences (excluding technical / mechanical skills)
63 completely, entirely
64 governing
65 threw off
66 foreign, alien
67 enraptured, carried away by excitement
68 entranced, ravished
69 (1) hidden, clandestine, (2) secluded, solitary (i.e., "magical")

Dost thou attend[70] me?

Miranda   Sir, most heedfully.

Prospero Being[71] once perfected[72] how to grant suits,[73]

80   How to deny them, who t' advance,[74] and who

To trash for over-topping[75] – new created[76]

The creatures[77] that were[78] mine, I say, or changed 'em,[79]

Or else new formed[80] 'em (having both the key[81]

Of officer and office),[82] set[83] all hearts i' th' state

85   To what[84] tune pleased his ear, that[85] now he was

The ivy which had hid[86] my princely trunk,

And sucked my verdure[87] out on't. – Thou attend'st not.

Miranda O good sir, I do.

Prospero   I pray thee, mark me.

I thus neglecting worldly ends,[88] all dedicated

---

70 listen/pay attention to★

71 my brother being

72 once perfected = now thoroughly accomplished/skilled in

73 petitions, requests

74 move forward, promote

75 trash for over-topping = retard/restrain/hold back (a hunting dog) for getting ahead of the pack

76 new created = and having newly elevated/appointed

77 human instruments

78 had been ("were": past tense)

79 changed 'em = substituted/exchanged one for another

80 shaped, trained, produced

81 (1) key to a lock, and (2) musical key for performers to play in

82 officer and office = minister/agent and job function

83 having placed/arranged ("place" also = [1] appointed, [2] fixed the musical key for performers)

84 whatever

85 so that

86 grown around and covered over

87 (1) fresh green color, (2) vitality

88 goals, purposes★

To closeness,[89] and the bettering of my mind 90
With that, which, but[90] by being so retired,[91]
O'er-prized all popular rate,[92] in my false brother
Awaked an evil nature, and my trust,
Like a good parent,[93] did beget of[94] him
A falsehood in its contrary[95] as great 95
As my trust was, which[96] had indeed no limit,
A confidence sans bound.[97] He being thus lorded,[98]
Not only with what my revenue yielded,[99]
But what my power might else exact,[100] like one
Who having into[101] truth, by telling of it,[102] 100
Made such a sinner of his memory
To credit[103] his own lie, he did believe
He was indeed the Duke, out o'[104] the substitution[105]
And executing[106] th' outward face of royalty

89 secrecy
90 except, aside from
91 secluded, withdrawn from worldly matters
92 o'er-prized all popular rate = exceeded the worth of all common/ordinary evaluation/opinion★
93 see the proverb invoked by Miranda in line 120
94 beget of = produce/create in
95 diametrically different/antithetical nature
96 his trust
97 sans bound = without boundaries/borders
98 given the role of/turned into a lord/ruler
99 not ONly WITH what MY reVENue YIELDed
100 eggZAKT (verb)
101 with reference to, against
102 his lie
103 to credit = in order to validate/make trustworthy★
104 out o' = from, because of
105 delegation of authority
106 and executing = and his performing/carrying out

105 With all prerogative.[107] Hence his ambition growing –
Dost thou hear?

Miranda   Your tale, sir, would cure deafness.[108]

Prospero To have no screen[109] between this part he played
And him he played it for,[110] he needs will be
Absolute Milan.[111] Me,[112] poor man, my library
110 Was dukedom large enough. Of temporal royalties[113]
He thinks me now incapable. Confederates,[114]
So dry[115] he was for sway,[116] wi' th' King of Naples
To give him annual tribute,[117] do him homage,
Subject his coronet[118] to his crown,[119] and bend[120]
115 The dukedom, yet[121] unbowed – alas, poor Milan! –
To most ignoble[122] stooping.

Miranda   O the heavens!

Prospero Mark his condition,[123] and th'event,[124] then tell me

---

107 all prerogative = all its rights/privileges
108 DOST thou HEAR your TALE sir WOULD cure DEAFness
109 partition, wall
110 him he played it for: Prospero
111 absolute Milan = completely the Duke (rulers were regularly referred to *as*
    the realm they governed: the King of France was called France, etc.)
112 but me, as for me
113 temporal royalties = worldly/secular ruling power/authority
114 (verb) he allies himself/conspires
115 desirous, thirsty
116 ruling power/authority
117 payment ("tax")
118 subordinate Antonio's/Milan's lesser/less powerful crown/realm
    (subJECT: verb)
119 his crown = the larger/more powerful crown/realm of Naples
120 bow
121 till then
122 dishonorable, base
123 his condition = the terms Antonio agreed to
124 what followed

If this might[125] be a brother.

Miranda   I should sin

To think but[126] nobly of my grandmother.[127]

Good wombs have borne bad sons.

Prospero   Now the condition.   120

This King of Naples being an enemy

To me inveterate,[128] hearkens[129] my brother's suit,

Which was, that he,[130] in lieu o'[131] the premises[132]

(Of homage, and I know not how much tribute)[133]

Should presently extirpate[134] me and mine   125

Out of the dukedom, and confer[135] fair[136] Milan,

With all the honors,[137] on my brother. Whereon[138]

A treacherous army[139] levied,[140] one midnight

Fated[141] to the purpose,[142] did Antonio open

The gates of Milan, and i' th' dead of darkness,   130

---

125 can
126 anything but, otherwise than
127 mother of both Prospero and Antonio
128 of long standing, firm, unswerving
129 listens* to (favorably: "gives him his ear")
130 the King of Naples
131 in lieu o' = in exchange / return for
132 the terms of their agreement
133 tax, penalty, homage money
134 presently extirpate = speedily / now* remove (exTIRpate)
135 bestow, grant
136 fine, handsome, lovely, beautiful*
137 rank, dignity
138 immediately
139 body / band of armed men (not the modern sense of a large, organized
       force)
140 raised
141 destined
142 matter in hand, object

The ministers[143] for th' purpose hurried thence
Me and thy crying self.

Miranda   Alack,[144] for pity.
I not rememb'ring how I cried out then
Will cry it o'er again. It is a hint[145]
That wrings[146] mine eyes to't.

135 Prospero   Hear a little further,
And then I'll bring[147] thee to the present business
Which now's upon us. Without the which this story
Were most impertinent.[148]

Miranda   Wherefore[149] did they not
That hour[150] destroy us?

Prospero   Well demanded,[151] wench.[152]
140 My tale provokes[153] that question. Dear, they durst not,
So dear the love my people bore me. Nor set[154]
A mark so bloody on the business, but
With colors[155] fairer, painted their foul[156] ends.
In few,[157] they hurried us aboard a bark,[158]

143 agents★
144 alas, for shame
145 occasion★
146 squeezes, presses
147 lead, conduct
148 irrelevant, out of place
149 why★
150 that hour = at that time
151 asked★
152 (1) girl, young woman★ (no negative senses), (2) my dear
153 invites, calls forth
154 nor set = nor did they dare place/put
155 qualities, characteristics
156 ugly, dirty, filthy★
157 brief ("a few words")
158 small ship

Bore us some leagues[159] to sea, where they prepared   145
A rotten carcass of a butt,[160] not rigged,[161]
Nor[162] tackle,[163] sail, nor mast. The very rats
Instinctively have[164] quit it. There they hoist[165] us
To cry to th' sea, that roared to us, to sigh
To th' winds, whose pity, sighing back again,   150
Did us but[166] loving wrong.[167]

Miranda   Alack, what trouble
Was I then to you?

Prospero   O, a cherubin[168]
Thou wast that did preserve[169] me. Thou didst smile,
Infused[170] with a fortitude[171] from heaven,
When[172] I have decked[173] the sea with drops full salt,   155
Under[174] my burden groaned,[175] which[176] raised in me
An undergoing stomach,[177] to bear up

159 1 league = approx. 3 mi.
160 cask ("tub")
161 having rigging: ropes of different thickness, for different purposes
162 neither
163 equipment, gear
164 had
165 set, put (raise up by means of tackle)
166 only
167 harm, injustice
168 angel
169 protect, keep alive
170 steeped, filled
171 strength, courage
172 on the occasions when
173 have decked = covered
174 when under
175 I groaned
176 her fortitude
177 courage / spirit★

Against what should[178] ensue.

Miranda   How came we ashore?

Prospero By Providence divine.[179]

160   Some food we had, and some fresh water, that

A noble Neapolitan, Gonzalo,

Out of his charity (who being then appointed

Master of this design[180]) did give us, with

Rich garments, linens, stuffs,[181] and necessaries

165   Which since have steaded[182] much, so of his gentleness[183]

Knowing I loved my books, he furnished me

From mine own library with volumes that

I prize above[184] my dukedom.

Miranda   Would I might

But ever[185] see that man.

Prospero   Now I arise.[186]

HE PUTS ON HIS MANTLE

170   Sit still, and hear the last of our sea-sorrow.

Here in this island we arrived, and here

Have I, thy schoolmaster, made thee more profit[187]

Than other princes can, that have more time[188]

---

178 what should = whatever might
179 Providence divine = provision/supply from God
180 scheme, plan
181 materials, stores, equipment
182 been advantageous/helpful
183 nobility of birth/breeding★
184 prize above = value/esteem★ more than
185 would I might but ever = I wish I could once/some time
186 (1) stand up (physical sense), (2) emerge from inactivity (psychological sense)
187 good, advantage★
188 leisure

For vainer[189] hours, and tutors[190] not so careful.[191]

Miranda Heavens thank you for't. And now I pray you sir, 175
    For still 'tis beating[192] in my mind, your reason
    For raising[193] this sea-storm?

Prospero   Know thus far forth.[194]
    By accident most strange, bountiful Fortune,[195]
    Now[196] my dear lady, hath mine enemies
    Brought to this shore. And by my prescience[197] 180
    I find my zenith[198] doth depend upon
    A most auspicious[199] star, whose influence
    If now I court[200] not, but omit,[201] my fortunes
    Will ever after droop.[202] Here cease more questions,
    Thou art inclined[203] to sleep. 'Tis a good dullness,[204] 185
    And give it way.[205] I know thou canst not choose.[206]

MIRANDA SLEEPS

189 less significant, more frivolous/futile
190 and tutors = than can tutors (hired teachers)
191 solicitous, attentive
192 throbbing, palpitating
193 causing, stirring up
194 thus far forth = this much
195 bountiful Fortune = the generous/graciously liberal goddess of luck/ chance★
196 now become (in contrast to before)
197 foreknowledge
198 (1) astrological highest point/culmination, (2) highest point of Fortune's turning wheel
199 promising, favorable
200 woo
201 neglect, fail to use★
202 sink down, descend
203 disposed, desirous
204 sluggishness, drowsiness, inertness
205 give it way = yield to it (give it the right of the road/way)
206 (i.e., his magic is involved; recall that he has again put on his magic mantle)

Come away,[207] servant, come! I am ready now,
Approach,[208] my Ariel. Come!

ENTER ARIEL

Ariel   All hail, great master, grave[209] sir, hail! I come
190   To answer thy best pleasure, be't[210] to fly,
        To swim, to dive into the fire, to ride
        On the curlèd[211] clouds. To thy strong bidding[212] task[213]
        Ariel and all his quality.[214]
    Prospero   Hast thou, spirit,
        Performed to point[215] the tempest that I bade thee?
195 *Ariel*   To every article.[216]
        I boarded the King's ship. Now on the beak,[217]
        Now in the waist,[218] the deck, in every cabin,
        I flamed amazement,[219] sometime I'd divide
        And burn in many places, on the topmast,
200   The yards and boresprit,[220] would I flame distinctly,[221]

---

207 come away = come from where you are to here
208 draw near
209 respected
210 be't = whether it be
211 spirally curved
212 strong bidding = powerful commands / orders
213 put to / assign work for (verb)
214 capacity, skill, natural characteristics★
215 performed to point = finished / carried through properly / completely / to
     the smallest detail★
216 item, matter
217 pointed prow
218 center of the upper deck
219 flamed amazement = blazed like fire and created frenzy / bewilderment /
     overwhelming fear
220 yards and boresprit = spars hung from the masts to support sails and
     bowsprit / large spar projecting from the front of the ship
221 separately, severally, individually

Then meet, and join. Jove's[222] lightning, the precursors[223]
O'th' dreadful thunderclaps, more momentary
And sight-outrunning[224] were not. The fire, and cracks[225]
Of sulfurous roaring,[226] the most mighty Neptune
Seem to besiege[227] and make his bold waves tremble,   205
Yea, his dread trident[228] shake.

Prospero   My brave spirit,
Who was so firm, so constant, that this coil[229]
Would not infect[230] his reason?

Ariel   Not a soul
But felt a fever of[231] the mad, and played
Some tricks[232] of desperation. All but mariners   210
Plunged in the foaming brine[233] and quit the vessel.
Then all afire with me the King's son Ferdinand
With hair up-staring[234] (then like reeds, not hair)
Was the first man that leapt, cried "Hell is empty,

222 chief of the gods in the Roman pantheon
223 heralds, forerunners
224 momentary and sight-outrunning = short-lived/transitory and faster than
     the eye could follow
225 loud booming
226 (since gunpowder emitted such fumes, it was thought that thunder did,
     too)
227 crowd around, attack ("the flames and loud booming seem to attack the
     profoundly powerful god of the sea, Neptune himself")
228 dread trident = dreaded/terrible three-pointed spear (Neptune's
     traditional sign, a fishing spear)
229 confusion, tumult
230 (1) affect, (2) corrupt, adulterate, injure
231 like that of
232 (1) freakish/foolish/ (2) craft/fraudulent actions*
233 salt/sea water* (it being a "desperate" act because most people, including
     most sailors, could not swim)
234 up-staring = standing on end

And all the devils are here.""

215 *Prospero*   Why that's my spirit.

But was not this nigh[235] shore?

Ariel   Close by, my master.

Prospero But are they, Ariel, safe?

Ariel   Not a hair perished.

On their sustaining garments[236] not a blemish,

But fresher[237] than before. And as thou bad'st me,

220 In troops[238] I have dispersed[239] them 'bout the isle.

The King's son have I landed by himself,

Whom I left cooling of the air[240] with sighs,

In an odd angle[241] of the isle, and sitting[242]

His arms in this (*he demonstrates*) sad[243] knot.

Prospero   .   Of the King's

ship,

225 The mariners,[244] say how thou hast disposed,[245]

And all the rest o' th' fleet?

Ariel   Safely in harbor

Is the King's ship, in the deep nook, where once

Thou call'dst me up at midnight to fetch dew[246]

235 near
236 sustaining garments: the clothing that, buoyed by trapped air (or by magic),
  kept them from sinking down in the water
237 cleaner, less stained / faded
238 groups
239 spread, scattered★
240 cooling of the air: by blowing on it, as he sighs?
241 odd angle = solitary corner
242 holding, keeping
243 weary, mournful
244 "the King's ship, and its sailors,"
245 placed, located, arranged
246 moisture,★ presumably for some magical purpose: midnight was considered
  a witching hour

From the still-vexed Bermoothes.[247] There she's[248] hid.
The mariners all[249] under hatches stowed,   230
Who, with a charm[250] joined to[251] their suffered labor,[252]
I have left asleep. And for[253] the rest o' th' fleet
(Which I dispersed) they all have met again,
And are upon the Mediterranean float[254]
Bound sadly home for Naples,   235
Supposing that they saw the King's ship wracked,
And his great person perish.

Prospero   Ariel, thy charge[255]
Exactly is performed, but there's more work.
What is the time o' th' day?

Ariel   Past the mid season.[256]

Prospero At least two glasses.[257] The time 'twixt six and now[258] 240
Must by us both be spent most preciously.[259]

Ariel   Is there more toil? Since thou dost give me pains,[260]
Let me remember[261] thee what thou hast promised,
Which is not yet performed me.[262]

247 still-vexed Bermoothes = always storm-afflicted Bermuda
248 the ship is
249 are all
250 magic spell★
251 joined to = combined with
252 their suffered labor = the exertion they endured
253 as for
254 waves, billows (Folio: flote)
255 task, commission
256 mid season = middle period/time
257 sand-filled hourglasses★
258 six and now = now and six o'clock
259 scrupulously, carefully
260 troubles, labors
261 recall to, remind
262 for me

Prospero   How now?[263]

    moody?[264]

    What is't thou canst demand?

245 Ariel   My liberty.

  Prospero Before the time be out?[265] No more!

  Ariel   I prithee,[266]

    Remember I have done thee worthy service,[267]

    Told thee no lies, made no mistakings, served

    Without or[268] grudge or grumblings. Thou didst promise

    To bate me[269] a full year.

250 Prospero   Dost thou forget

    From what a torment I did free thee?

  Ariel   No.

  Prospero Thou dost. And think'st it much[270] to tread the ooze[271]

    Of the salt deep,

    To run upon the sharp wind of the north,

255   To do me business in the veins[272] o' th' earth

    When it is baked[273] with frost.

  Ariel   I do not, sir.

  Prospero Thou liest, malignant[274] thing! Hast thou forgot

---

263 what?★

264 stubborn, arrogant, sullen

265 be out = is up

266 I pray you: I earnestly / humbly ask★

267 worthy service = excellent★ work, employment★

268 either

269 bate me = reduce / lessen★ my time of service

270 a lot / great deal

271 tread the ooze = walk along the slimy bottom

272 seams, channels, fissures

273 hardened

274 rebellious, malcontent

The foul witch Sycorax,[275] who with[276] age and envy[277]
Was grown[278] into a hoop?[279] Hast thou forgot her?

Ariel   No, sir.   260

Prospero Thou hast. Where was she born? Speak, tell me.

Ariel   Sir, in Argier.[280]

Prospero   O, was she so? I must
Once in a month recount what thou hast been,
Which thou forget'st. This damned[281] witch Sycorax
For mischiefs[282] manifold, and sorceries terrible   265
To enter[283] human hearing, from Argier
Thou know'st was banish'd. For one thing she did[284]
They would not take her life. Is not this true?

Ariel   Ay, sir.

Prospero This blue-eyed[285] hag[286] was hither brought with   270
child,[287]
And here was left by the sailors. Thou my slave,[288]
As thou report'st thyself, wast then her servant,
And for[289] thou wast a spirit too delicate[290]

---

275 SIKorAX
276 because of, from
277 malevolence★
278 was grown = grew
279 circle
280 Algiers, in N. Africa
281 (1) condemned to eternal punishment, by God, *or* (2) condemned by the
     Algerian authorities
282 evil deeds, crimes
283 come into
284 one thing she did: become pregnant, which ruled out capital punishment
285 blue-eyed = having blue eyelids: a sign of pregnancy
286 demon, witch
287 with child = pregnant
288 (1) servant without rights or freedom,★ (2) rascal★
289 because
290 (1) tender, soft, (2) fastidious, dainty, exquisite★

To act[291] her earthy and abhorred[292] commands,[293]
275   Refusing her grand hests,[294] she did confine[295] thee
By help of her more potent[296] ministers,
And in her most unmitigable[297] rage,
Into a cloven[298] pine, within which rift[299]
Imprisoned, thou didst painfully remain
280   A dozen years, within which space[300] she died,
And left thee there, where thou didst vent[301] thy groans
As fast as mill-wheels[302] strike. Then was this island
(Save for the son, that she did litter[303] here,
A freckled whelp,[304] hag-born) not honored[305] with
A human shape.

285 *Ariel*   Yes. Caliban her son.
  Prospero Dull[306] thing, I say[307] so. He, that Caliban
Whom now I keep in service. Thou best know'st
What torment I did find thee in, thy groans
Did make wolves howl, and penetrate the breasts

291 perform, do
292 earthy and abhorred = gross/coarse and disgusting/horrifying★
293 to ACT her EARTHy AND abHORRED comMANDS
294 grand hests = (1) large, (2) principal orders/commands
295 imprison
296 powerful★
297 unappeasable (unMItiGAble)
298 split lengthwise
299 cleft, fissure★
300 time
301 discharge, express, pour out
302 mill-wheels = waterwheels, used to power grain-grinding mills
303 give birth to (used for animals and, with people, contemptuously)
304 freckled whelp = spotted young animal/puppy
305 graced, adorned
306 stupid
307 said

Of ever-angry bears. It was a torment 290
To lay upon the damned, which Sycorax
Could not again undo. It was mine art,
When I arrived, and heard thee, that made gape
The pine, and let thee out.

Ariel   I thank thee, master.

Prospero If thou more murmur'st,[308] I will rend[309] an oak[310] 295
And peg[311] thee in his[312] knotty entrails till
Thou hast howled away twelve winters.

Ariel   Pardon, master.
I will be correspondent to command[313]
And do my spriting,[314] gently.[315]

Prospero   Do so. And after two days
I will discharge[316] thee.

Ariel   That's my noble master! 300
What shall I do? Say what? What shall I do?

Prospero Go make thyself like a nymph o' th' sea, be subject
To no sight but thine and mine — invisible
To every eyeball else. Go take this shape,
And hither come in 't. Go! Hence! With diligence![317] 305

EXIT ARIEL

308 more murmur'st = any more/again complain/grumble
309 tear open, cleave
310 (much denser and harder than pine)
311 fasten
312 its
313 correspondent to command = agreeable/answerable to authority/the
       giving of orders
314 acting as a sprite/spirit
315 courteously, in subdued/quiet fashion
316 free
317 speed

(*to Miranda*) Awake, dear heart awake, thou hast slept well,
Awake.

Miranda   (*waking*) The strangeness of your story put
Heaviness[318] in me.

Prospero   Shake it off. Come on,
We'll visit Caliban, my slave, who never
Yields[319] us kind[320] answer.

310 Miranda   'Tis a villain,[321] sir,
I do not love to look on.

Prospero   But as 'tis
We cannot miss[322] him. He does make our fire,
Fetch in our wood, and serves in offices
That profit us. What ho! slave! Caliban!
Thou earth,[323] thou! Speak.

315 Caliban   (*within*) There's wood enough
within.

Prospero Come forth, I say, there's other business for thee.
Come thou tortoise! When?

ENTER ARIEL AS A WATER NYMPH

(*to Ariel*) Fine apparition.[324] My quaint[325] Ariel,
Hark[326] in thine ear.

318 drowsiness
319 gives
320 (1) proper, fitting, well-bred, (2) natural, good, (3) sympathetic, gentle
321 base-minded peasant scoundrel
322 go/do without★
323 dirt, dust
324 fine apparition = a superior★ (1) semblance/illusion/appearance, (2)
     specter/phantom
325 ingenious, clever, skillful
326 listen

PROSPERO WHISPERS IN ARIEL'S EAR

Ariel   My lord, it shall be done.

EXIT ARIEL

Prospero (*to Caliban*) Thou poisonous slave, got[327] by the Devil   320
  himself
  Upon thy wicked dam,[328] come forth!

ENTER CALIBAN

Caliban As wicked dew,[329] as e'er my mother brushed
  With raven's[330] feather from unwholesome fen[331]
  Drop on you both! A south-west[332] blow on ye,
  And blister you all o'er!   325
Prospero For this be sure, tonight thou shalt have cramps,
  Side-stitches that shall pen[333] thy breath up, urchins[334]
  Shall for that vast[335] of night that they may work
  All exercise[336] on thee. Thou shalt be pinched
  As thick as honeycomb,[337] each pinch more stinging   330
  Than bees that made 'em.

---

327 begot, conceived
328 female parent (used largely for animals)
329 as wicked dew = may a dew as wicked
330 black crowlike bird of ill omen
331 unwholesome fen = noxious marsh-muck/mold*
332 winds associated with unhealthily warm and damp weather
333 close, shut
334 goblins, elves (since the word also means "hedgehog," the goblins
    themselves may be in that shape)
335 great/long time
336 work all exercise = busy themselves
337 honeycomb: a model of compact density

Caliban   I must eat[338] my dinner.
This island's mine by Sycorax my mother,
Which thou tak'st from me. When thou cam'st first
Thou strok'st me, and made much of me. Wouldst[339] give me
335   Water with berries in't. And teach me how
To name the bigger light,[340] and how[341] the less
That burn by day and night.[342] And then I loved thee,
And showed thee all the qualities o' th' isle,
The fresh springs,[343] brine-pits,[344] barren place,[345] and
fertile.[346]
340   Cursed be I that did so! All the charms
Of Sycorax, toads, beetles, bats, light[347] on you![348]
For I am all the subjects that you have,
Which first was mine own king. And here you sty[349] me
In this hard rock,[350] whiles you do keep from me
The rest o' th' island.
345   *Prospero*   Thou most lying slave,

338   go and eat
339   wouldst (thou wouldst) = you would
340   bigger light = the sun
341   how to name
342   the less that burn by day and night = the lesser lights – stars, the moon (the
       latter frequently still visible during the day, even to our electricity-dazzled
       eyes)
343   water sources/streams*
344   salt pits
345   places
346   those places that are fertile
347   descend
348   of SYcorAX toads BEEtles BATS light ON you (prosodic scansion, *not*
       pronunciation/reading)
349   confine/pen up, as in a pigsty
350   Prospero's cell, too, is apparently a rock cave

Whom stripes[351] may move,[352] not kindness! I have used[353] thee,
Filth as thou art, with humane[354] care, and lodged thee
In mine own cell, till thou didst seek to violate
The honor of my child.

Caliban Oh ho, oh ho, would't had been done!   350
Thou didst prevent me, I had peopled[355] else
This isle with Calibans.

Miranda   Abhorrèd slave,
Which[356] any print[357] of goodness wilt not take,
Being capable of all ill.[358] I pitied thee,
Took pains to make thee speak, taught thee each hour   355
One thing or other. When thou didst not, savage,
Know thine own meaning, but wouldst gabble like
A thing most brutish, I endowed thy purposes[359]
With words that made them known. But thy vile[360] race,[361]
Though thou didst learn, had that in't which good natures   360
Could not abide[362] to be with. Therefore wast thou
Deservedly confined into this rock, who hadst
Deserved more than a prison.

Caliban You taught me language, and my profit on't

351 blows, lashes
352 (1) affect, rouse, ★ (2)trouble, perturb
353 treated★
354 HYUmane
355 populated
356 who
357 stamp, impression
358 wickedness, depravity★
359 endowed thy purposes = enriched your objects/goals★
360 Folio: vild
361 vile race = disgusting/depraved tribe/people
362 continue, endure★

365   Is, I know how to curse. The red plague[363] rid you
    For learning me your language!

Prospero   Hag-seed,[364] hence!
    Fetch us in fuel, and be quick thou 'rt best,
    To answer[365] other business. Shrug'st thou, malice?
    If thou neglect'st, or dost unwillingly

370   What I command, I'll rack thee with old[366] cramps,
    Fill all thy bones with aches,[367] make thee roar,
    That beasts shall tremble at thy din.

Caliban   No, pray thee.
    (*aside*) I must obey. His art is of such power,
    It would control my dam's god Setebos,[368]
    And make a vassal[369] of him.

375 *Prospero*   So slave, hence!

EXIT CALIBAN

ENTER FERDINAND, AND ARIEL, INVISIBLE,
PLAYING AND SINGING

Ariel
    Come unto these yellow sands,
      And then take hands.
    Curtsied when you have, and kissed
      The wild waves whist,[370]

380   Foot it featly[371] here and there,

363 red plague = (?) a disease producing sores or bleeding
364 hag-seed = witch-child
365 accomplish, act as directed
366 (1) abundant, plentiful, (2) familiar
367 EYchiz
368 a Patagonian demon (SEteBOS)
369 servant, subordinate
370 silent (adjective)
371 elegantly, properly★

And sweet sprites the burden[372] bear.[373]
    Hark, hark!

(*burden: bow, wow, dispersedly*[374])

The watch dogs bark.

(*burden: bow, wow, dispersedly*)   385

Hark, hark, I hear
The strain[375] of strutting Chanticleer[376]
Cry "Cock-a-diddle-dow"
Ferdinand Where should[377] this music be? I' th' air or th' earth?
It sounds[378] no more. And sure it waits upon[379]   390
Some god o' th' island. Sitting on a bank,
Weeping again the King my father's wrack,
This music crept by me upon the waters,[380]
Allaying both their fury and my passion[381]
With its sweet air.[382] Thence I have followed it   395
(Or it hath drawn me rather), but 'tis gone.
No, it begins again.
Ariel   (*sings*) Full fathom[383] five thy father lies,

372 refrain
373 carry
374 from all over
375 song
376 crowing rooster / cock
377 must
378 resounds, is played / sung
379 waits upon = is intended for / in service to
380 this MUsic CREPT by ME upON the WAters
381 painful suffering
382 tune, melody, song★
383 Folio: fadom (1 fathom = 6 feet)

Of his bones are coral made.
400 Those are pearls that were his eyes,
Nothing of him that doth fade
But doth suffer[384] a sea-change
Into something rich, and strange.
Sea-nymphs hourly ring his knell.

405 (*burden: Ding-dong*)

Hark now I hear them, ding-dong, bell.
Ferdinand The ditty[385] does remember[386] my drownèd
father.[387]
This is no mortal business, nor no sound
That the earth owes.[388] I hear it now above me,
410 *Prospero* (*to Miranda*) The fringèd curtains[389] of thine eye
advance,[390]
And say what thou seest yond.[391]
Miranda   What is't, a spirit?
Lord, how it looks about. Believe me, sir,
It carries a brave form.[392] But 'tis a spirit.

384 nothing of him that doth fade / but doth suffer = all the parts of him that
vanish (except his bones) undergo
385 song
386 recall the memory, commemorate
387 *either* the DITty DOES reMEMber my DROWNed FAther *or* the DITty
DOES reMEMber MY drowned FAther
388 possesses, owns★
389 fringèd curtains = eye lids
390 move upward, raise★
391 yonder
392 carries a brave form = exhibits / displays a handsome / fine shape / body

Prospero No wench, it eats, and sleeps, and hath such senses
   As we have. Such.[393] This gallant[394] which thou see'st   415
   Was in the wrack. And but[395] he's something[396] stained
   With grief – that's beauty's canker[397] – thou mightst call him
   A goodly[398] person. He hath lost his fellows[399]
   And strays[400] about to find 'em.

Miranda   I might call him
   A thing divine, for nothing natural[401]   420
   I ever saw so noble.

Prospero   (*aside*) It goes on[402] I see
   As my soul prompts[403] it. Spirit, fine spirit, I'll free thee
   Within two days for this.

Ferdinand   (*seeing Miranda*) Most sure, the[404]
   goddess
   On whom these airs attend.[405] Vouchsafe[406] my prayer[407]
   May know[408] if you remain[409] upon this island,   425

393 just so, exactly
394 fine gentleman
395 and but = except that
396 somewhat★
397 (1) ulcer, sore, (2) disease
398 (1) good-looking, handsome, (2) excellent, admirable★
399 companions★
400 wanders, roams
401 formed by Nature
402 goes on = proceeds, happens ("it" is often regarded as referring to
     Prospero's plan/scheme, but the reference may be to "things" – the flow
     and movement of existence)
403 urges, suggests
404 this is the
405 are in service
406 grant
407 request, supplication, entreaty
408 may know = that I may learn/be made aware/find out
409 abide, dwell

And that you will some good instruction give
How I may bear me here. My prime request
(Which I do last pronounce)[410] is (O you wonder!)[411]
If you be maid[412] or no?

Miranda   No wonder sir,
But certainly a maid.

430 Ferdinand   My language?[413] Heavens!
I am the best of them that speak this speech,
Were I but where 'tis spoken.

Prospero   (to Ferdinand) How? The best?
What wert[414] thou if the King of Naples heard thee?

Ferdinand   A single[415] thing, as I am now, that wonders
435 To hear thee speak of Naples. He[416] does hear me,
And that he does, I weep. Myself am Naples,
Who, with mine eyes (never since at ebb)[417] beheld
The King my father wracked.

Miranda   Alack, for[418] mercy!

Ferdinand   Yes faith,[419] and all his lords, the Duke of
Milan
And his brave son[420] being twain.[421]

---

410 utter, speak
411 Italian "mirando" = wonderful, marvelous"
412 an unmarried / virginal woman, not pledged in marriage
413 not only was there no "Italy," but neither was there an "Italian" language;
    large dialectal variations remain to this day
414 would you be ("what would happen to you")
415 solitary
416 the King of Naples: Ferdinand believes his father dead and himself
    succeeded to the throne
417 at ebb = dry
418 out of consideration for
419 faith / in faith / i'faith = indeed
420 Antonio's son is never again mentioned in the play
421 two of them

Prospero   (aside) The Duke of   440
Milan[422]
And his more braver[423] daughter could control[424] thee,
If now 'twere fit to do't. At the first sight
They have changed eyes. Delicate Ariel,
I'll set thee free for this. (to Ferdinand) A word, good sir.
I fear you have done yourself some wrong.[425] A word!   445
Miranda   (aside) Why speaks my father so ungently?[426] This
Is the third man[427] that e'er I saw, the first
That e'er I sighed for. Pity[428] move my father
To be inclined my way!
Ferdinand   O, if a virgin,
And your affection[429] not gone forth,[430] I'll make you   450
The Queen of Naples.
Prospero   Soft[431] sir, one word more.
(aside) They are both in either's[432] powers. But this swift
Business I must uneasy[433] make, lest too light[434] winning
Make the prize light. (to Ferdinand) One word more. I
charge[435] thee

422 himself
423 more braver = finer, better
424 rebuke, take to task, challenge
425 harm (by calling himself King of Naples, and for the "spying" Prospero
      goes on to allege)
426 rudely, discourteously, roughly
427 her father, Ferdinand, and Caliban
428 may pity
429 emotional disposition★
430 gone forth = been given elsewhere/to someone else
431 slowly
432 each other's
433 uncomfortable, hard, troublesome
434 slight, trivial, cheap★
435 command★

455 That thou attend me. Thou dost here usurp
The name thou ow'st not, and hast put thyself
Upon this island as a spy, to win it
From me, the lord on't.[436]

Ferdinand   No, as I am a man.

Miranda   There's nothing ill can dwell in such a temple.[437]

460 If the ill spirit have so fair a house,
Good things will strive to dwell with't.

Prospero   (to Ferdinand) Follow
me.
(to Miranda) Speak not you for him. He's a traitor.
(to Ferdinand) Come,
I'll manacle thy neck and feet together.
Seawater shalt thou drink. Thy food shall be
465 The fresh-brook mussels, withered roots, and husks[438]
Wherein the acorn cradled.[439] Follow.

Ferdinand   No,
I will resist such entertainment,[440] till
Mine enemy has more power.

HE DRAWS HIS SWORD, AND IS MAGICALLY
PREVENTED FROM MOVING

Miranda   O dear father,
Make not too rash[441] a trial[442] of him, for

436 of it
437 human body (in Christian belief, inhabited by the divine spirit)
438 the dry outer sheaths
439 lay, grew
440 treatment
441 hasty
442 test*

He's gentle, and not fearful.

Prospero   What, I say,   470
My foot[443] my tutor?[444] Put thy sword up,[445] traitor,
Who mak'st a show, but dar'st not strike, thy conscience
Is so possessed with guilt. Come, from thy ward,[446]
For I can here disarm thee with this stick,[447]
And make thy weapon drop.

Miranda   Beseech[448] you, father!   475

Prospero Hence! Hang not on my garments.

Miranda   Sir, have pity,
I'll be his surety.[449]

Prospero   Silence! One word more
Shall make me chide[450] thee, if not hate thee. What,
An advocate[451] for an impostor? Hush![452]
Thou think'st there is no more such shapes[453] as he,   480
Having seen but him and Caliban. Foolish wench,
To[454] the most of men this is a Caliban,
And they to him are angels.

Miranda   My affections
Are then most humble. I have no ambition

---

443 my foot = someone so far beneath me
444 guide, teacher
445 put up thy sword = sheathe (pack up / stow away) your sword
446 from thy ward = away from your guardian / protector (i.e., Miranda: an insulting sneer)
447 his magic wand
448 I beg
449 guarantor, warrantor
450 be angry, scold
451 an advocate = you'll be a defender
452 an ADvoCET for AN imPOStor HUSH
453 bodily appearances
454 compared to

485   To see a goodlier man.

    Prospero   (*to Ferdinand*) Come on, obey.

    Thy nerves[455] are in their infancy again,

    And have no vigor[456] in them.

    Ferdinand   So they are.

    My spirits, as in a dream, are all bound up.

490   My father's loss, the weakness which I feel,

    The wrack of all my friends, nor this man's threats,

    To whom I am subdued, are but light to me,

    Might I but through my prison once a day

    Behold this maid. All corners else o' th' earth

495   Let liberty make use of. Space enough

    Have I in such a prison.

    Prospero   (*aside*) It works. (*to Ferdinand*) Come

    on.

    (*aside*) Thou hast done well, fine Ariel! (*to Ferdinand*) Follow

    me.

    (*to Ariel*) Hark what thou else shalt do me.

    Miranda   (*to Ferdinand*) Be

    of comfort,

    My father's of a better nature, sir,

500   Than he appears by speech. This is unwonted[457]

    Which now[458] came from him.

    Prospero   (*to Ariel*) Thou shalt be as

    free

    As mountain winds. But then[459] exactly do

455 sinews, muscles
456 strength
457 unusual, not common
458 just now
459 until then

All points of my command.

Ariel   To th' syllable.[460]

Prospero (*to Ferdinand*) Come, follow. (*to Miranda*) Speak not for
him.

EXEUNT

---

460 least portion/smallest part of a word

Act 2

❦

Another part of the Island

ENTER ALONSO, SEBASTIAN, ANTONIO, GONZALO,
ADRIAN, FRANCISCO, AND OTHERS

Gonzalo (*to Alonso*) Beseech you, sir, be merry. You have cause
　　(So have we all) of joy, for our escape
　　Is much beyond[1] our loss. Our hint of woe
　　Is common,[2] every day:[3] some sailor's wife,
5　　The masters[4] of some merchant, and the merchant
　　Have just our theme of woe. But for the miracle
　　(I mean our preservation) few in millions
　　Can speak like us. Then wisely, good sir, weigh
　　Our sorrow with our comfort.
Alonso　　　　　　　　　　　Prithee peace.[5]

1 surpassing, greater
2 ordinary, plain, humble★
3 every day = daily (syntactically in apposition to "common," rather than
　introductory to "some sailor's wife," etc.)
4 sea captains
5 be silent

44

Sebastian (*to Antonio, aside*) He receives comfort like cold   10
    porridge.

Antonio   The visitor[6] will not give him o'er so.[7]

Sebastian   Look, he's winding up the watch of his wit, by and by[8]
    it will strike.[9]

Gonzalo   Sir –   15

Sebastian   One. Tell.[10]

Gonzalo   When every grief is entertained[11] that's offered,
    Comes[12] to the entertainer[13] –

Sebastian   A dollar.

Gonzalo   Dolor[14] comes to him indeed. You have spoken truer   20
    than you purposed.[15]

Sebastian   You have taken it wiselier[16] than I meant you should.

Gonzalo   Therefore my lord –

Antonio   Fie, what a spendthrift[17] is he of his tongue.

Alonso   I prithee spare.[18]   25

Gonzalo   Well, I have done. But yet –

Sebastian   He will be talking.

Antonio   Which, of[19] he or Adrian, for a good wager, first

---

6 charity / comfort-giving person
7 thus, in that style / fashion
8 soon, at once★
9 (1) sound, as clocks did, striking the hour, (2) hit
10 count (as in "bank teller")
11 accepted
12 there comes
13 (1) recipient, (2) host, as at an inn, (3) giver of public entertainment
14 pain, suffering
15 meant to
16 as more sensible / acute
17 waster, prodigal consumer
18 refrain, forbear
19 either

      begins to crow?

30 *Sebastian* The old cock.

    Antonio The cockerel.[20]

    Sebastian Done. The wager?

    Antonio A laughter.[21]

    Sebastian A match.[22]

35 *Adrian* Though this island seem to be desert – [23]

    Sebastian Ha, ha, ha! So. You're paid.

    Adrian Uninhabitable, and almost inaccessible –

    Sebastian Yet –

    Adrian Yet –

40 *Antonio* He could not miss it.

    Adrian It must needs be of subtle, tender, and delicate
      temperance.[24]

    Antonio Temperance[25] was a delicate wench.

    Sebastian Ay, and a subtle,[26] as he most learnedly delivered.[27]

45 *Adrian* The air breathes[28] upon us here most sweetly.

    Sebastian As if it had lungs, and rotten[29] ones.

    Antonio Or, as 'twere perfumed by a fen.[30]

---

20 young cock
21 (?) it is not clear who is to laugh or why
22 a match = an agreement ("agreed")
23 (adjective) deserted, uninhabited
24 subtle, tender, and delicate temperance = fine, soft, and pleasant/delightful
    climate
25 a woman's name, common among English Puritans
26 cunning, crafty, sly
27 stated, uttered★
28 blows softly
29 (1) putrid, decayed, (2) unsound, weak (the word "tuberculosis" was not then
    in use, but the disease was well known – indeed, Europeans brought it to the
    New World, until then free of it)
30 marsh

Gonzalo Here is everything advantageous[31] to life.

Antonio True, save[32] means to live.

Sebastian Of that there's none, or little.   50

Gonzalo How lush and lusty[33] the grass looks! how green!

Antonio The ground indeed[34] is tawny.[35]

Sebastian With an eye[36] of green in't.

Antonio He misses not much.

Sebastian No. He doth but[37] mistake the truth totally.   55

Gonzalo But the rarity[38] of it is, which is indeed almost beyond
  credit – [39]

Sebastian As many vouched[40] rarities are.

Gonzalo That our garments being, as they were, drenched in
  the sea, hold notwithstanding[41] their freshness and glosses,[42]   60
  being rather new-dyed than stained with salt water.

Antonio If but one of his pockets[43] could speak, would it not
  say he lies?

Sebastian Ay, or very falsely pocket up his report.

Gonzalo Methinks our garments are now as fresh as when we   65
  put them on first in Afric, at the marriage of the King's fair
  daughter Claribel to the King of Tunis.

31 favorable, useful
32 other than, except
33 lush and lusty = soft/luxuriant and (1) pleasant/beautiful, (2) vigorous
34 ground indeed = soil/earth in truth
35 brownish
36 tinge, slight shade, spot
37 doth but = just
38 unusualness
39 belief
40 asserted, claimed, guaranteed
41 nevertheless, in spite of that
42 luster
43 small pouches/bags worn inside (or attached to) clothing

Sebastian 'Twas a sweet marriage, and we prosper well[44] in our
return.

70 *Adrian* Tunis was never graced before with such a paragon
to[45] their queen.

Gonzalo Not since widow Dido's time.[46]

Antonio Widow? A pox o' that. How came that widow in?
Widow Dido!

75 *Sebastian* What if he had said widower Aeneas too? Good Lord,
how you take[47] it!

Adrian Widow Dido said you? You make me study of[48] that.
She was of Carthage, not of Tunis.

Gonzalo This Tunis, sir, was[49] Carthage.[50]

80 *Adrian* Carthage?

Gonzalo I assure you, Carthage.

Antonio His word is more[51] than the miraculous harp.[52]

Sebastian He[53] hath raised[54] the wall, and houses too.

Antonio What impossible matter will he make easy next?

85 *Sebastian* I think he will carry this island home in his pocket,
and give it his son for an apple.

---

44 prosper well = flourish, thrive
45 paragon to = model of excellence as
46 Dido, Queen of Carthage, was indeed a widow, but is not usually so talked
of: her tragic affair with the Trojan prince Aeneas has been what history has
focused on
47 deal with, treat, understand
48 study of = think about
49 was once
50 Carthage (destroyed by Rome in 146 B.C.E.) was then (and is now) Tunisia
51 more powerful
52 with which magical harp, Amphion built the walls of Thebes
53 Gonzalo
54 made, brought into existence, produced★

Antonio   And sowing the kernels[55] of it in the sea, bring forth
more islands.

Gonzalo   Ay.

Antonio   Why, in good time.   90

Gonzalo   (*to Alonso*) Sir, we were talking, that our garments
seem now as fresh as when we were at Tunis at the marriage
of your daughter, who is now Queen.

Antonio   And the rarest[56] that e'er came there.

Sebastian   Bate,[57] I beseech you, widow Dido.   95

Antonio   O widow Dido? Ay, widow Dido.

Gonzalo   Is not sir my doublet as fresh as the first day I wore it?
I mean, in a sort.[58]

Antonio   That sort[59] was well fished for.

Gonzalo   When I wore it at your daughter's marriage.   100

Alonso   You cram[60] these words into mine ears against
The stomach of my sense.[61] Would I had never
Married my daughter there! For coming thence
My son is lost, and (in my rate) she too,
Who is so far from Italy removed   105
I ne'er again shall see her. O thou mine heir
Of Naples and of Milan! What strange fish
Hath made his meal on thee?

Francisco   Sir, he may live,

55 seeds
56 most exceptional queen
57 (1) let's leave out/omit/have an end to, (2) except
58 in a sort = after a fashion, more or less
59 (?) sword, meaning swordfish?
60 stuff, pack
61 the stomach of my sense = the desire/inclination/state of my mind

I saw him beat[62] the surges[63] under him,
110   And ride upon their backs. He trod the water
Whose enmity[64] he flung aside, and breasted[65]
The surge most swoll'n that met him. His bold head
'Bove the contentious[66] waves he kept, and oared
Himself with his good arms in lusty stroke
115   To th' shore, that o'er his[67] wave-worn basis[68] bowed,
As[69] stooping to relieve him.[70] I not doubt
He came alive to land.

Alonso   No, no, he's gone.

Sebastian Sir, you may thank yourself for this great loss,
That would not bless our Europe with your daughter,
120   But rather lose her to an African,[71]
Where she at least is banished from your eye
Who hath cause[72] to wet the grief on't.[73]

Alonso   Prithee peace.

Sebastian You were kneeled to, and importuned otherwise
By all of us. And the fair soul herself
125   Weighed[74] between loathness,[75] and obedience, at

62 hit, thrash
63 waves
64 ill-will, hostility, hatred
65 faced, opposed
66 quarrelsome, warlike
67 its (the shore's)
68 foundation
69 as if
70 relieve him = rescue / help / assist Ferdinand
71 (not a racial remark: North Africans were considered Caucasians)
72 who hath cause = who (his daughter) has reason
73 wet the grief on't = bedew with weeping the sadness / sorrow of it
74 weighed between = balanced / compared / measured / considered
75 reluctance

Which end o' th' beam[76] should bow.[77] We have lost your
son,
I fear forever. Milan and Naples have
More widows in them of this business' making,
Than we bring men to comfort them.
The fault's your own.

Alonso   So is the dearest of the loss.   130

Gonzalo   My lord Sebastian,
The truth you speak doth lack some gentleness,
And time[78] to speak it in. You rub the sore,
When you should bring the plaster.[79]

Sebastian   Very well.

Antonio   And most chirurgeonly.[80]   135

Gonzalo   (to Alonso) It is foul weather in us all, good sir,
When you are cloudy.[81]

Sebastian   Fowl weather?

Antonio   Very foul.

Gonzalo   Had I plantation[82] of this isle, my lord –

Antonio   He'd sow 't[83] with nettle-seed.[84]

Sebastian   Or docks, or
mallows.[85]

---

76 the balance beam of the scale
77 bend★ (rhymes with "so, go," etc.)
78 proper/appropriate time
79 healing/soothing application
80 spoken like a medical man (Gonzalo is not a surgeon: there seems to be no
    more than that in the remark)
81 darkened (by negative matters)
82 had I plantation = if I had colonization/settlement
83 plantation can also refer to planting
84 stinging weeds
85 docks, or mallows = dock weeds or other common weeds

140 *Gonzalo*   And were the king on't,[86] what would I do?

Sebastian   'Scape[87] being drunk, for want[88] of wine.

Gonzalo   I' the commonwealth[89] I would by contraries[90]

Execute[91] all things. For no kind of traffic[92]

Would I admit.[93] No name of magistrate.[94]

145 Letters[95] should not be known. Riches, poverty,

And use of service, none. Contract, succession,[96]

Bourn,[97] bound[98] of land, tilth,[99] vineyard,[100] none.

No use of metal, corn, or wine, or oil.

No occupation.[101] All men idle,[102] all.

150 And women too, but innocent and pure.

No sovereignty[103] –

Sebastian   Yet he would be king on't.

Antonio   The latter end of his commonwealth forgets the

beginning.

Gonzalo   All things in common[104] nature should produce

---

86 were the king on't = if I were the king of it
87 avoid, be freed from
88 lack
89 matters of public good / concern
90 by contraries = very differently
91 perform, carry out ("do")
92 commerce
93 permit, allow
94 government officials
95 (1) literature, (2) learning
96 inheritance
97 boundaries
98 landmarks establishing boundaries
99 agricultural work
100 cultivation of vineyards
101 jobs, occupations
102 not working
103 rank, domination, authority
104 in common = of a general / universal

Without sweat or endeavor. Treason, felony,
Sword, pike,[105] knife, gun, or need of any engine[106]   155
Would I not have. But nature should bring forth
Of it own kind,[107] all foison,[108] all abundance,
To feed my innocent people.

Sebastian No marrying 'mong his subjects?

Antonio None, man, all idle – whores and knaves.   160

Gonzalo I would with such perfection govern, sir,
To excel[109] the Golden Age.[110]

Sebastian Save[111] his Majesty!

Antonio Long live Gonzalo!

Gonzalo And – do you mark me, sir?   165

Alonso Prithee no more. Thou dost talk nothing[112] to me.

Gonzalo I do well believe your Highness, and did it to minister
occasion[113] to these gentlemen, who are of such sensible and
nimble[114] lungs, that they always use to[115] laugh at nothing.

Antonio 'Twas you we laughed at.   170

Gonzalo Who, in this kind of merry fooling am[116] nothing to
you. So you may continue, and laugh at nothing still.

Antonio What a blow was there given!

---

105 a kind of spear
106 tools, implements, machines, weapons
107 of itself ("naturally")
108 abundance, plenty (FOYzin)*
109 to excel = so as to surpass
110 a historical myth about the glories of early humanity
111 may God protect
112 trivialities, insignificance, meaninglessness
113 minister occasion = furnish opportunity/excuse
114 sensible and nimble = effective/sensitive and agile/swift
115 always use to = always are in the habit of/accustomed to
116 am as

Sebastian An[117] it had not fallen flat-long.[118]

175 *Gonzalo* You are gentlemen of brave mettle.[119] You would lift the moon out of her sphere,[120] if she would continue in it five weeks without changing.

ENTER ARIEL, INVISIBLE, PLAYING SOLEMN MUSIC

Sebastian We would so, and then go a-bat-fowling.[121]

Antonio (*to Gonzalo*) Nay good my lord, be not angry.

180 *Gonzalo* No, I warrant you, I will not adventure my discretion[122] so weakly.[123] Will you laugh me asleep, for I am very heavy?

Antonio Go sleep, and hear[124] us.

ALL SLEEP BUT ALONSO, SEBASTIAN, AND ANTONIO

Alonso What, all so soon asleep? I wish mine eyes

185 Would (with[125] themselves) shut up my thoughts. I find They are inclined to do so.

Sebastian   Please you, sir, Do not omit the heavy offer[126] of it. It seldom visits sorrow. When it doth, It is a comforter.

117 if
118 flat on its face
119 temperament, spirit
120 according to Ptolemaic astronomy, all heavenly bodies (stars, planets, moons, etc.) were contained within spheres (transparent hollow globes), but "sphere" was coming to mean "orbit"
121 catching birds roosting, at night
122 adventure my discretion = commit/risk/endanger my judgment
123 so weakly = with such lack of mental firmness
124 listen to
125 by
126 sleep being "heavy," its proffer of itself must also be "heavy"

Antonio　　　　　　　We two my lord,
　Will guard your person while you take your rest,　　　　　190
　And watch your safety.
Alonso　　　　　　　　Thank you. Wondrous heavy!

ALONSO SLEEPS

EXIT ARIEL

Sebastian What a strange drowsiness possesses them!
Antonio　　It is the quality o' th' climate.
Sebastian　　　　　　　　　　Why
　Doth it not then our eyelids sink? I find not
　Myself disposed[127] to sleep.　　　　　　　　195
Antonio　　Nor I, my spirits are nimble.
　They fell[128] together all, as by consent[129]
　They dropped,[130] as by a thunder-stroke. What might,[131]
　Worthy Sebastian? O, what might? No more.[132]
　And yet, methinks I see it in thy face,　　　　　200
　What thou should'st[133] be. The occasion speaks[134] thee, and
　My strong[135] imagination sees a crown
　Dropping upon thy head.
Sebastian　　　　　　What? Art thou waking?[136]
Antonio　　Do you not hear me speak?

127 inclined, in the mood to
128 came (naturally), passed, rushed
129 as if by general agreement
130 dropped: an extension of the metaphoric "fell"; *not* literally "dropping"
131 might be
132 no more = I'll say no more
133 ought to, might
134 speaks to (in the sense of revealing, proclaiming)
135 (1) robust, fertile, intense, vivid, (2) courageous, brave, (3) tenacious
136 awake

Sebastian   I do, and surely

205 It is a sleepy language, and thou speak'st

Out of[137] thy sleep. What is it thou didst say?

This is a strange repose, to be asleep

With eyes wide open. Standing, speaking, moving,

And yet so fast[138] asleep.

Antonio   Noble Sebastian,

210 Thou let'st thy fortune sleep. Die, rather. Wink'st[139]

Whiles thou art waking.

Sebastian   Thou dost snore distinctly:[140]

There's meaning in thy snores.

Antonio   I am more serious[141] than my custom.[142] You

Must be so too, if[143] heed me. Which to do[144]

Trebles thee o'er.[145]

215 *Sebastian*   Well. I am standing water.[146]

Antonio   I'll teach[147] you how to flow.

Sebastian   Do so. To ebb[148]

Hereditary sloth[149] instructs me.

Antonio   O!

137 out of = from
138 soundly, firmly
139 close/shut your eyes,* disregard
140 plainly, clearly
141 earnest, solemn*
142 habitual practice
143 if you
144 to do = if you do
145 trebles thee o'er = multiplies/increases you threefold/three times over ("triples you")
146 standing water = water that is stagnant/not ebbing or flowing
147 show, guide, inform
148 flow backwards, recede
149 sluggishness, laziness

If you but knew how you the purpose cherish[150]
Whiles thus you mock it. How[151] in stripping[152] it
You more invest[153] it. Ebbing men, indeed   220
(Most often) do so near the bottom run
By[154] their own fear or sloth.

Sebastian   Prithee say on.
The setting[155] of thine eye and cheek proclaim
A matter[156] from thee, and a birth,[157] indeed,
Which throes[158] thee much to yield.[159]

Antonio   Thus sir.   225
Although this lord[160] of weak remembrance,[161] this
Who shall be of as[162] little memory
When he is earthed,[163] hath here almost persuaded
(For he's a spirit of persuasion, only
Professes to[164] persuade) the King his son's alive,   230
'Tis as impossible that he's undrowned
As he that sleeps here swims.[165]

---

150 the purpose cherish = caress / cultivate / make much of the goal / desired
    object
151 if you only knew how
152 (1) unclothing, revealing, (2) avoiding, moving away from
153 clothe, adorn
154 because of
155 manner
156 subject matter
157 (1) bringing forth, origin, (2) bulk, weight
158 pains
159 produce, put forth, deliver, allow
160 Gonzalo
161 memory
162 equally
163 buried
164 professes to = declares* himself in order to
165 is at the same time swimming

Sebastian   I have no hope[166]
     That he's undrowned.
Antonio   O, out of that no hope
     What great hope have you! No hope that way, is
235 Another way so high a hope, that even
     Ambition cannot pierce a wink[167] beyond
     But doubts discovery[168] there. Will you grant[169] with me
     That Ferdinand is drowned?
Sebastian   He's gone.
Antonio   Then tell me,
     Who's the next heir of Naples?[170]
Sebastian   Claribel.
240 Antonio   She that is Queen of Tunis. She that dwells
     Ten leagues beyond man's[171] life. She that from Naples
     Can have no note,[172] unless the sun were post[173]
     (The Man i' th' Moon's too slow)[174] till[175] newborn chins
     Be[176] rough and razorable. She that from whom[177]
245 We all were sea-swallowed, though some cast[178] again,

166 (1) expectation, (2) desire
167 quick glance
168 doubts discovery = is uncertain/hesitant that revelation/information
     will/can be
169 agree
170 (1) Alonso, (2) the kingdom itself (see Sebastian's comment in lines 250–
     252)
171 human, civilized
172 written comment
173 the early form of mail was, by horse or coach, from one "post" (for
     changing horse[s]) to another
174 i.e., the sun takes a single day to complete his circuit; the moon takes 28
     days
175 till the time that it takes for
176 to be/become
177 she that from whom = she who away from whom
178 some were cast up

And by[179] that destiny[180] to perform an act
Whereof[181] what's past is prologue, what to come
In yours, and my, discharge.[182]

Sebastian What stuff[183] is this? How say you?
    'Tis true my brother's daughter's Queen of Tunis,   250
    So[184] is she heir of Naples, 'twixt which regions
    There is some space.[185]

Antonio   A space whose every cubit[186]
    Seems to cry out "How shall that Claribel
    Measure us[187] back to Naples? Keep[188] in Tunis,
    And let Sebastian wake." Say this[189] were death   255
    That now hath seized them,[190] why they were[191] no worse
    Than now they are. There be that[192] can rule Naples
    As well as he[193] that sleeps, lords that can prate[194]
    As amply and unnecessarily
    As this Gonzalo. I myself could make[195]   260

---

179 because of
180 fact, course of events, predetermined fortune
181 by means of which
182 fulfillment, performance, execution
183 what stuff = (1) what's this all about, (2) what nonsense/rubbish
184 therefore, thus
185 distance (space also = time, but Antonio's response indicates that distance
    is here at issue)
186 1 cubit = approx. 18 inches
187 measure us = travel over all the cubits
188 stay
189 suppose ("say for the sake of argument") this sleep
190 Alonso, Gonzalo, etc.
191 would be
192 those that/who
193 Alonso
194 chatter, blabber
195 turn out, train (some editors explain as "turn myself into")

A chough[196] of as deep chat.[197] O, that you bore[198]
The mind that I do, what a sleep were this
For your advancement![199] Do you understand me?

Sebastian Methinks I do.

Antonio   And how does your content[200]
Tender[201] your own good fortune?

265 *Sebastian*   I remember
You did supplant[202] your brother Prospero.

Antonio   True.
And look how well my garments[203] sit upon me,
Much feater than before. My brother's servants
Were then my fellows, now they are my men.[204]

270 *Sebastian* But for your conscience –

Antonio   Ay, sir. Where lies that?[205] If 'twere a kibe,[206]
'Twould put me to[207] my slipper. But I feel not[208]
This deity[209] in my bosom. Twenty consciences
That stand 'twixt[210] me and Milan, candied be they[211]

---

196 crow, jackdaw (CHUFF)
197 as deep chat = equally extensive / comprehensible / weighty chatter /
     prattle / small talk
198 had, harbored (a CHUFF of AS deep CHAT o THAT you BORE)
199 advance / promotion to higher rank
200 pleasure (conTENT: note that the prosody helps identifying this as
     "conTENT" rather than KONtent)
201 relate to, regard (either positively or negatively)
202 (use of the intensifier "did" here makes "supplant" a good deal stronger)
203 (clothes then *were* the man / woman: people were identifiable by what they
     could afford – and were by law permitted – to wear)
204 servants
205 lies that = is that located
206 chapped / ulcerated sore / chilblain on the heel
207 put me to = force me into
208 feel not = cannot find / touch / perceive
209 divine characteristic (sarcastic reference to conscience)
210 between
211 candied be they = may they be preserved by boiling in sugar

And melt ere they molest![212] Here lies your brother,   275
No better than the earth he lies upon,
If he were that which now he's like[213] (that's dead),
Whom I, with this obedient steel — three inches of it —
Can lay to bed forever, whiles you doing (*he gestures*) thus,
To the perpetual[214] wink for aye[215] might put   280
This ancient morsel,[216] this Sir Prudence, who
Should not upbraid our course.[217] For[218] all the rest[219]
They'll take suggestion[220] as a cat laps milk,
They'll tell the clock to any business[221] that
We say befits[222] the hour.

Sebastian   Thy case, dear friend,   285
Shall be my precedent. As[223] thou got'st Milan,
I'll come by Naples. Draw thy sword, one stroke
Shall free thee from the tribute which thou pay'st,[224]
And I the King shall love thee.

Antonio   Draw together,
And when I rear[225] my hand, do you the like   290
To fall it[226] on Gonzalo.

212 cause trouble / grief / vexation
213 he's like = he looks like
214 eternal, permanent
215 ever
216 tidbit, choice dish
217 upbraid our course = censure / criticize our behavior / conduct / way of
    acting
218 as for
219 rest of them
220 a hint
221 activity, matter, piece of work
222 is suitable / proper for
223 exactly / just as
224 to Alonso
225 raise
226 fall it = let your sword descend / drop

Sebastian	O, but one word.

THE Y MOVE TO THE SIDE AND TALK, INAUDIBLY

MUSIC. ENTER ARIEL, INVISIBLE

Ariel   (*to Gonzalo*) My master through his art foresees the
        danger
    That you, his friend, are in, and sends me forth
    (For else his project[227] dies) to keep thee living.

ARIEL SINGS IN GONZALO'S EAR

295   While you here do snoring lie,
        Open-eyed conspiracy[228]
            His time[229] doth take.
        If of life you keep a care,[230]
        Shake off slumber and beware.
300   Awake, awake!

ANTONIO AND SEBASTIAN RESUME THEIR PRIOR PLACES

Antonio   Then let us both be sudden.

Gonzalo   (*waking*) Now, good
        angels
        Preserve the King!

THE OTHERS WAKE UP

Alonso   Why how now, ho! Awake? Why are you drawn?
        Wherefore this ghastly looking?

Gonzalo   What's the matter?

227 plan, scheme★
228 conSPIraSIGH
229 the favorable occasion/opportunity★
230 concern, solicitude

Sebastian Whiles we stood here securing[231] your repose,   305
  Even[232] now, we heard a hollow[233] burst of bellowing
  Like bulls, or rather lions, did't not wake you?
  It struck mine ear most terribly.

Alonso   I heard nothing.

Antonio O, 'twas a din to fright a monster's ear,
  To make an earthquake. Sure it was the roar   310
  Of a whole herd of lions.

Alonso   Heard you this, Gonzalo?

Gonzalo Upon mine honor, sir, I heard a humming,
  And that a strange one too, which did awake me.
  I shaked you, sir, and cried. As mine eyes opened,
  I saw their weapons drawn. There was a noise,   315
  That's verily.[234] 'Tis best we stand upon our guard,
  Or that we quit this place. Let's draw our weapons.

Alonso Lead off[235] this ground and let's make further search
  For my poor son.

Gonzalo   Heavens keep him from these beasts!
  For he is sure i' th' island.

Alonso   Lead away.   320

EXEUNT

Ariel Prospero my lord shall[236] know what I have done:
  So, King, go safely on to seek thy son.

EXIT

231 guarding, protecting
232 precisely, exactly
233 strangely empty-sounding (?)
234 a fact, true
235 you go first and conduct/lead us away from
236 must

SCENE 2

Another part of the Island

ENTER CALIBAN, WITH A LOAD OF WOOD
A NOISE OF THUNDER IS HEARD

Caliban All the infections[1] that the sun sucks up
　　From bogs,[2] fens, flats,[3] on Prosper fall, and make him
　　By inchmeal[4] a disease! His spirits hear me,
　　And yet I needs must curse. But they'll nor[5] pinch,
5　　Fright me with urchin-shows,[6] pitch[7] me i' the mire,[8]
　　Nor lead me like[9] a firebrand, in the dark
　　Out of my way, unless he bid 'em. But
　　For every trifle are they set upon me,
　　Sometime like apes[10] that mow[11] and chatter at me,
10　　And after bite me. Then like hedgehogs, which
　　Lie tumbling[12] in my barefoot way, and mount[13]
　　Their pricks[14] at my foot-fall. Sometime am I
　　All wound[15] with adders,[16] who with cloven[17] tongues

1 contamination / corruption via air or water
2 spongy wet ground
3 level country
4 little by little, by inches
5 neither
6 displays of goblins and elves
7 throw, cast
8 swampy / boggy ground
9 in the guise of
10 monkeys★
11 make faces / grimaces (rhymes with "cow")★
12 rolling
13 lift, raise
14 sharp needle-like spines
15 WOWND (adjective)
16 snakes, serpents
17 split

Do hiss me into madness.

        Lo, now lo,

Here comes a spirit of his, and to torment[18] me   15
For bringing wood in slowly. I'll fall flat;
Perchance[19] he will not mind[20] me.

Trinculo Here's neither bush nor shrub[21] to bear[22] off any
weather[23] at all, and another storm brewing, I hear it sing i'
th' wind. Yond same[24] black cloud, yond huge one, looks like   20
a foul bombard[25] that would[26] shed his liquor. If it should
thunder, as it did before, I know not where to hide my head.
Yond same cloud cannot choose but fall by pailfuls. (*notices
Caliban*) What have we here? A man or a fish? Dead or alive?
A fish, he smells like a fish. A very ancient and fish-like smell,   25
a kind of not-of-the-newest Poor-John.[27] A strange fish!
Were I in England now (as once I was), and had but this fish
painted,[28] not a holiday fool[29] there but would give a piece
of silver.[30] There would this monster make a man.[31] Any

18 plague, trouble
19 perhaps
20 notice, perceive
21 bush nor shrub = small, compact shrubs close to the ground nor shrubs less
    large than trees
22 keep, hold
23 unsettled / stormy weather
24 one and the same, identical, very
25 leather jug / bottle for liquor (usage derived from "bombard," an early form
    of cannon)
26 would like to
27 salted, dried fish
28 portrayed on a signboard, to advertise a performance
29 holiday fool = a fool on holiday
30 piece of silver = silver coin
31 make a man = make a fortune for a man

30   strange beast there makes a man. When[32] they will not give a
doit[33] to relieve[34] a lame beggar, they will lay out ten to see a
dead Indian. Legged[35] like a man, and his fins like arms.
(*touches Caliban*) Warm o' my troth.[36] I do now let loose[37]
my opinion, hold it no longer, this is no fish, but an islander,
35   that hath lately suffered[38] by a thunderbolt.[39]

THUNDER

Alas, the storm is come again. My best way is to creep under
his gabardine.[40] There is no other shelter hereabout. Misery
acquaints[41] a man with strange bedfellows. I will here
shroud[42] till the dregs[43] of the storm be past.

TRINCULO CRAWLS UNDER CALIBAN'S GABARDINE
ENTER STEPHANO WITH A BOTTLE IN HIS HAND, SINGING

40   *Stephano*   I shall no more to sea, to sea,
                Here shall I die a-shore.
This is a very scurvy[44] tune to sing at a man's funeral. Well,
here's my comfort.

HE DRINKS, THEN SINGS

32 whereas
33 small coin, of Dutch origin (DOYT)
34 aid, help
35 having legs (monosyllabic)
36 o' my troth = really, indeed, actually
37 let loose = give up, abandon
38 been afflicted/struck
39 lightning
40 loose upper garment of coarse cloth
41 introduces, makes known
42 take shelter
43 falling moisture
44 contemptible, worthless, shabby★

The master, the swabber,[45] the boatswain and I,
　　The gunner,[46] and his mate,[47]　　　　　　　　　　　　　45
Mall, Meg, and Marian, and Margery,
　　But none of us cared for Kate.
For she had a tongue with a tang,[48]
Would cry to a sailor "Go hang!"
She loved not the savor[49] of tar nor of pitch,　　　　　　　50
Yet a tailor[50] might scratch her where'er she did itch.
Then to sea boys, and let her go hang.
　This is a scurvy tune too. But here's my comfort.

HE DRINKS

Caliban　Do not torment me. O!

Stephano　What's the matter?[51] Have we devils here? Do you put　　45... 55
tricks upon us with salvages[52] and men of Ind?[53] Ha! I have
not 'scaped drowning, to be afeard now of your four legs.[54]
For it hath been said,[55] "As proper[56] a man as ever went on
four legs[57] cannot make him give ground." And it shall be
said so again, while Stephano breathes at 's[58] nostrils.　　　　60

45 seaman who cleans/washes the decks
46 cannoneer
47 assistant
48 sting
49 aroma, smell
50 tailors were often made fun of, among other things for being unmanly (see
　King Lear, 2.2.60)
51 what's the matter = what's up, what's going on
52 savages
53 probably the West Indies, but the word is also applied to India
54 two are Caliban's, two are Trinculo's
55 proverbially
56 good, perfect
57 proverbially: *two* legs
58 at's = at/through his

Caliban The spirit torments me. O!

Stephano This is some monster of the isle with four legs, who hath got (as I take[59] it) an ague.[60] Where the devil should[61] he learn our language? I will give him some relief if it be but
65 for that.[62] If I can recover[63] him, and keep him tame, and get to Naples with him, he's a present for any emperor that ever trod on neat's[64]-leather.

Caliban Do not torment me, prithee. I'll bring my wood home faster.

70 *Stephano* He's in his fit[65] now and does not talk after the wisest.[66] He shall taste of[67] my bottle. If he have never drunk wine afore, it will go near to remove[68] his fit. If I can recover him, and keep him tame, I will not take too much[69] for him. He shall pay for him that hath[70] him, and that soundly.[71]

75 *Caliban* Thou dost me yet[72] but little hurt. Thou wilt anon,[73] I know it by thy trembling. Now Prosper works upon[74] thee.

Stephano Come on your ways.[75] Open your mouth. Here is that

59 suppose, think
60 acute/violent fever, with accompanying shaking (EYgyuw)
61 could/might
62 if it be but for that = if that's all it is
63 heal, restore, cure
64 oxlike
65 fit of convulsions
66 after the wisest = according to good sense
67 from
68 go near to remove = come pretty close to removing
69 I will not take too much = they won't be able to pay me too much ("the sky's the limit")
70 gets
71 thoroughly, to the full
72 as yet
73 immediately, instantly
74 on
75 come on your ways = come along/on (ways = paths, roads)

which will give language to you,[76] cat. Open your mouth,
this will shake[77] your shaking, I can tell you, and that soundly.
(*Caliban drinks*) You cannot tell who's your friend, open your   80
chaps again.

Trinculo   I should[78] know that voice. It should be – but he is
drowned, and these are devils. O defend me.

Stephano   Four legs and two voices, a most delicate monster. His
forward[79] voice now is to speak well of his friend, his   85
backward[80] voice is to utter foul speeches, and to detract.[81] If
all the wine in my bottle will recover him, I will help his
ague. Come. Amen,[82] I will pour some in thy other mouth.

Trinculo   Stephano!

Stephano   Doth thy other mouth call me? Mercy, mercy. This is a   90
devil, and no monster. I will leave him, I have no long
spoon.[83]

Trinculo   Stephano! If thou beest[84] Stephano, touch me, and
speak to me for I am Trinculo. Be not afeared – thy good
friend Trinculo.   95

Stephano   If thou beest Trinculo, come forth. I'll pull thee by the
lesser[85] legs. (*he starts to pull*) If any be Trinculo's legs, these
are they. Thou art very Trinculo indeed. How cam'st thou to

---

76 to you = even to you (proverb: "Good liquor will make a cat speak")
77 get rid of ("shake off")
78 ought to
79 front
80 back
81 criticize, disparage, speak evil of
82 an appreciative if blasphemous comment on Caliban having taken a good
   long drink
83 "He that sups with the devil needs a long spoon" (proverb)
84 BEEST (be-est)
85 smaller

be the siege[86] of this moon-calf?[87] Can he vent[88] Trinculos?

100 *Trinculo* I took him to be killed with[89] a thunderstroke. But art thou not drowned, Stephano? I hope now thou are not drowned. Is[90] the storm overblown?[91] I hid me under the dead moon-calf's gabardine for fear of the storm. And art thou living, Stephano? O Stephano, two Neapolitans 'scaped!

TRINCULO CAPERS ABOUT, THEN TRIES TO PULL
STEPHANO INTO HIS DANCE

105 *Stephano* Prithee, do not turn me about,[92] my stomach is not constant.[93]

Caliban (*aside*) These be fine things,[94] an if[95] they be not sprites. That's a brave god, and bears celestial liquor. I will kneel to him.

110 *Stephano* How didst thou 'scape? How cam'st thou hither? Swear by this bottle how thou cam'st hither. I escaped upon a butt of sack,[96] which the sailors heaved overboard, by[97] this bottle — which I made of the bark of a tree, with mine own hands, since I was cast ashore.

115 *Caliban* I'll swear upon that bottle to be thy true subject, for the liquor is not earthly.

86 excrement
87 moon-calf = misshapen birth, monstrosity
88 defecate
89 took him to be killed with = supposed he'd been killed by
90 has
91 blown over
92 around
93 steady
94 entities, creatures
95 an if = if
96 white wine
97 I swear by

Stephano Here, (*he gives Trinculo the bottle*) swear then how thou
  escapedst.

Trinculo (*drinking and passing the bottle back*) Swum ashore, man,
  like a duck. I can swim like a duck, I'll be sworn.   120

Stephano Here, kiss the book.[98] (*passes the bottle again*) Though
  thou canst swim like a duck, thou art made like a goose.[99]

Trinculo O Stephano, hast any more of this?

Stephano The whole butt, man. My cellar[100] is in a rock by the
  seaside, where my wine is hid. (*to Caliban*) How now, moon-   125
  calf? How does thine ague?

Caliban Hast thou not dropped from heaven?

Stephano Out o' the moon, I do assure thee. I was the Man in
  the Moon, when time was.[101]

Caliban I have seen thee in her,[102] and I do adore thee, my   130
  mistress[103] showed me thee, and thy dog and thy bush.[104]

Stephano Come, swear to that. Kiss the book. I will furnish it
  anon with new contents. Swear.

Trinculo By this good light, this is a very shallow[105] monster. I
  afeard of him? A very weak monster. The Man i' the Moon?   135
  A most poor credulous monster. Well drawn,[106] monster, in
  good sooth.

---

98 (i.e., demonstrate that you do indeed swear – though it is the Bible men so
    kissed – by drinking)
99 Trinculo is starting to wobble, because of the wine
100 wine cellar
101 when time was = once upon a time
102 the moon
103 female counterpart of "master"
104 the man had been banished to the moon, either for stealing wood or for
    gathering it on a Sunday; the thornbush represents that wood
105 superficial, slight
106 well drawn = a good pull / drink

Caliban   I'll show thee every fertile inch o' the island. And I
will kiss thy foot. I prithee, be my god.

140 *Trinculo*   By this light,[107] a most perfidious[108] and drunken
monster: when his god's asleep, he'll rob his bottle.

Caliban   I'll kiss thy foot. I'll swear myself thy subject.

Stephano   Come on then. Down[109] and swear.

Trinculo   I shall laugh myself to death at this puppy-headed
145 monster. A most scurvy monster. I could find in my heart to
beat him, –

Stephano   Come, kiss.

Trinculo   But[110] that the poor monster's in drink.[111] An
abominable[112] monster.

150 *Caliban*   I'll show thee the best springs. I'll pluck thee berries.
I'll fish for thee, and get thee wood enough.
A plague upon the tyrant that I serve,
I'll bear him no more sticks, but follow thee,
Thou wondrous man.

155 *Trinculo*   A most ridiculous monster, to make a wonder of a
poor drunkard.

Caliban   I prithee let me bring thee where crabs grow,
And I with my long nails will dig thee pig-nuts,[113]
Show thee a jay's nest, and instruct thee how
160 To snare the nimble marmozet. I'll bring thee
To clust'ring filberts,[114] and sometimes I'll get thee

---

107 the sun: they swear by anything and everything, except God
108 treacherous, faithless
109 get down
110 except
111 in drink = drunk
112 loathsome, disgusting, detestable
113 peanuts
114 hazelnuts

Young scamels[115] from the rock. Wilt thou go with me?

Stephano I prithee now lead the way without any more talking.
Trinculo, the king, and all our company else being drowned,
we will inherit here. (*to Caliban*) Here, bear my bottle. Fellow   165
Trinculo, we'll fill him[116] by and by again.

Caliban (*singing drunkenly*) Farewell master, farewell, farewell!

Trinculo A howling monster, a drunken monster.

Caliban (*sings*)
No more dams I'll make for fish,
Nor fetch in firing,[117]   170
At requiring,[118]
Nor scrape trenchering,[119] nor wash dish,
'Ban 'Ban, Ca-Caliban,
Has a new master, get a new man.
Freedom, high-day,[120] high-day freedom, freedom, high-day,   175
freedom!

Stephano O brave monster, lead the way.

EXEUNT

115 (?) some form of barnacle or other ocean dweller?
116 it (the bottle)
117 firewood
118 at requiring = on demand
119 trenchering = wooden platters ("trenchers"), later replaced by plates
120 day of high celebration

Act 3

SCENE I

The Island

ENTER FERDINAND, CARRYING A LOG

Ferdinand There be some sports[1] are painful,[2] and their labor
Delight in them sets off.[3] Some kinds of baseness[4]
Are nobly undergone, and most poor matters[5]
Point[6] to rich ends. This my mean[7] task
5   Would be as heavy[8] to me, as odious,[9] but
The mistress which I serve quickens[10] what's dead,
And makes my labors pleasures. O she is
Ten times more gentle than her father's crabbèd,[11]

---

1 entertainments, pastimes
2 are painful = which are toilsome/laborious
3 sets off = balances out
4 lowliness, characteristics of low birth
5 activities, circumstances
6 are directed/aimed
7 inferior, low
8 weighty ("difficult"), oppressive
9 repulsive, disagreeable
10 animates, gives life to
11 disagreeable, cross, ill-tempered

And he's composed[12] of harshness. I must remove
Some thousands of these logs, and pile them up,   10
Upon a sore injunction.[13] My sweet mistress[14]
Weeps when she sees me work, and says such baseness
Had never like executor.[15] I forget.[16]
But these sweet thoughts do even refresh my labors,
Most busy least when I do it.[17]

ENTER MIRANDA. PROSPERO, UNSEEN, IS BEHIND HER

Miranda   Alas, now pray you,   15
    Work not so hard. I would[18] the lightning had
    Burnt up those logs that you are enjoined[19] to pile!
    Pray set it down, and rest you. When this burns
    'Twill weep for having wearied you. My father
    Is hard at study, pray now rest yourself,   20
    He's safe[20] for these three hours.
Ferdinand   O most dear mistress,
    The sun will set before I shall discharge
    What I must strive to do.
Miranda   If you'll sit down
    I'll bear your logs the while. Pray give me that,
    I'll carry it to the pile.
Ferdinand   No, precious creature,   25

12 made of
13 sore injunction = severe order
14 lady love★
15 like executor = such a performer/agent/worker
16 am forgetting (his work)
17 most busy least = so that I am in truth least actively engaged in these mean
    labors when I am actually doing them (and thinking those sweet thoughts)
18 wish
19 ordered, commanded
20 out of harm's way

I had rather crack my sinews,[21] break my back,
Than you should such dishonor[22] undergo,
While I sit lazy by.

Miranda   It would become[23] me
As well as it does you, and I should do it
30   With much more ease, for my good will is to it,
And yours it is against.[24]

Prospero   (*aside*) Poor worm[25] thou art
infected,
This visitation[26] shows it.

Miranda   You look wearily.[27]

Ferdinand No, noble mistress, 'tis fresh morning with me
When you are by at night. I do beseech you –
35   Chiefly that I might set[28] it in my prayers –
What is your name?

Miranda   Miranda. O my father,
I have broke your hest[29] to say so.[30]

Ferdinand   Admired Miranda,[31]
Indeed the top[32] of admiration, worth
What's dearest to the world! Full many a lady

21 muscles*
22 shame, disgrace
23 suit, be appropriate for
24 and YOURS it's aGAINST
25 small creature (here affectionate, since he speaks of Miranda)
26 (1) visit, (2) visit of inspection, in times of plague / general infection
27 look wearily = seem / appear weary
28 place, put
29 command, bidding
30 say so = speak thus (telling her name)
31 admired = wondered at / wonderful ("miranda," in Latin and Italian = wonderful)
32 height

I have eyed[33] with best regard,[34] and many a time   40
The harmony[35] of their tongues hath into bondage
Brought my too diligent[36] ear. For several virtues[37]
Have I liked several women, never any
With so full soul[38] but some defect in her
Did quarrel[39] with the noblest grace she owed,   45
And put it to the foil.[40] But you, O you,
So perfect, and so peerless, are created
Of every creature's best.

Miranda   I do not know
One of my sex, no woman's face remember,
Save from my glass[41] mine own. Nor have I seen   50
More that I may call men, than you good friend,
And my dear father. How features[42] are abroad[43]
I am skilless[44] of, but by my modesty
(The jewel in my dower)[45] I would not wish
Any companion in the world but you.   55
Nor can imagination[46] form a shape

33 looked at
34 (1) observant attention, (2) evaluation, respect
35 pleasing quality
36 attentive
37 several virtues = various/different/distinct★ (1) qualities, (2) moral
   characteristics
38 so full soul = such (1) overwhelming emotion (on his part) or (2) a
   complete/perfect sensibility/nature (on her part)
39 conflict (verb)
40 repulse, check, defeat
41 mirror ("looking glass")
42 faces
43 in the outside world
44 ignorant
45 natural endowment
46 my imagination

Besides yourself, to like of. But I prattle
Something too wildly,[47] and my father's precepts[48]
I therein do forget.

Ferdinand   I am, in my condition[49]

60   A prince, Miranda, I do think a king
(I would not so) and would no more endure
This wooden[50] slavery than to suffer
The fleshfly blow[51] my mouth. Hear my soul speak.
The very instant that I saw you, did

65   My heart fly to your service, there resides
To make me slave to it,[52] and for your sake
Am I this patient log-man.

Miranda   Do you love me?

Ferdinand O heaven! O earth! Bear witness to this sound,
And crown what I profess with kind event[53]

70   If I speak true. If hollowly,[54] invert[55]
What best is boded[56] me, to mischief.[57] I,
Beyond all limit of what else i'[58] the world,
Do love, prize, honor you.

Miranda   I am a fool
To weep at what I am glad of.

47 aimlessly, confusedly, without order
48 instructions, orders
49 position, status
50 (1) graceless, inferior, (2) involving wood
51 fleshfly blow = maggots to breed*
52 your service
53 happening, occurrence
54 if hollowly = if I speak insincerely
55 subvert, reverse
56 foretold, proclaimed
57 misfortune, harm, evil*
58 is in

Prospero	(*aside*) Fair encounter

Of two most rare affections. Heavens rain grace   75
On that which breeds[59] between 'em.

Ferdinand	Wherefore weep you?

Miranda   At mine unworthiness, that dare not offer
What I desire to give, and much less take
What I shall die to want.[60] But this is trifling,[61]
And all the more it[62] seeks to hide itself,   80
The bigger bulk it shows.[63] Hence, bashful cunning,[64]
And prompt[65] me, plain and holy innocence!
I am your wife, if you will marry me.
If not, I'll die your maid.[66] To be your fellow[67]
You may deny me, but I'll be your servant,   85
Whether you will or no.

Ferdinand	My mistress dearest,

And I thus humble ever.

Miranda	My husband then?

Ferdinand Ay, with a heart as willing[68]
As bondage e'er[69] of freedom. Here's my hand.

Miranda   And mine, with my heart in't. And now farewell   90
Till half an hour hence.

59 develops
60 lack, miss
61 foolish / frivolous talk
62 the trifling
63 the underlying metaphor is pregnancy, which cannot (after a time) be denied
64 craftiness, artifice
65 (1) incite, (2) assist
66 (1) maidservant, (2) virgin
67 equal, companion
68 wishing, wanting, desiring
69 ever is

Ferdinand   A thousand thousand![70]

Prospero   So glad of this as they I cannot be,
        Who[71] are surprised with all.[72] But my rejoicing
        At nothing can be more. I'll to my book,[73]
95   For yet ere supper time, must I perform
        Much business appertaining.[74]

                    EXIT

70 a thousand thousand = a million farewells
71 they who
72 with all = by everything (some editors emend Folio "with all" to "withal,"
    meaning "by it")
73 book of magic
74 proper, relevant

SCENE 2

Another part of the Island

ENTER CALIBAN, STEPHANO, AND TRINCULO

Stephano (*to Trinculo*) Tell not me,[1] when the butt is out[2] we will
drink water, not a drop before. Therefore bear up, and board
'em,[3] servant monster, drink to me.

Trinculo Servant monster? The folly[4] of this island![5] They say
there's but five[6] upon this isle. We are three of them, if th'   5
other two be brained[7] like us, the state totters.

Stephano Drink, servant monster when I bid thee, thy eyes are
almost set[8] in thy head.

Trinculo Where should they be set else? He were a brave
monster indeed if they were set in his tail.   10

Stephano My man monster hath drowned his tongue in sack. For
my part[9] the sea cannot drown me, I swam ere I could
recover the shore, five-and-thirty leagues off and on, by this
light thou shalt be my lieutenant monster, or my standard.[10]

Trinculo Your lieutenant if you list,[11] he's no standard.[12]   15

---

1 tell not me = don't tell me (to be more careful about preserving our wine
supply)
2 empty
3 bear up, and board 'em = (literally) sail right up for the attack, boarding
another ship, meaning here "drink up"
4 foolishness, insanity
5 Folio: comma after "island"; all editors emend
6 i.e., these three plus Prospero and Miranda
7 be brained = have minds/brains
8 fixed, glazed
9 share, portion, side★
10 standard-bearer, ensign
11 like, wish
12 (1) flag, banner, (2) bearer of anything, since he's too drunk to stand up

Stephano We'll not run,[13] Monsieur monster.

Trinculo Nor go neither. But you'll lie[14] like dogs, and yet say
nothing neither.

Stephano Moon-calf, speak once in thy life, if thou beest a good
20 moon-calf.

Caliban How does thy honor? Let me lick thy shoe.
(*indicating Trinculo*) I'll not serve him, he is not valiant.

Trinculo Thou liest most ignorant monster, I am in case to
justle[15] a constable.[16] Why, thou deboshed[17] fish thou, was
25 there ever man a coward, that hath drunk so much sack as I
today? Wilt thou tell a monstrous lie, being but half a fish,
and half a monster?

Caliban Lo, how he mocks me, wilt thou let[18] him my lord?

Trinculo Lord, quoth[19] he? That a monster should be such a
30 natural![20]

Caliban Lo, lo again. Bite him to death I prithee.

Stephano Trinculo, keep a good tongue in your head. If you
prove[21] a mutineer, the next tree![22] The poor monster's my
subject, and he shall not suffer indignity.

35 *Caliban* I thank my noble lord. Wilt thou be pleased
To hearken once again to the suit I made to thee?

---

13 run from the enemy, in battle
14 (1) lie down, (2) tell lies
15 in case to justle = in a state / condition to joust / fight with, knock around
16 military / peace officer
17 debauched = depraved, corrupt
18 (1) stop, (2) permit, allow
19 says
20 half-wit (monster = *un*natural)
21 turn out to be★
22 the next tree = I'll hang you to the next tree

Stephano Marry²³ will I. Kneel, and repeat it. I will stand, and so
shall Trinculo.

ENTER ARIEL, INVISIBLE

Caliban As I told thee before, I am subject to a tyrant,
A sorcerer, that by his cunning hath   40
Cheated me of the island.

Ariel   Thou liest.

Caliban (*to Trinculo*) Thou liest, thou jesting monkey, thou.
I would my valiant master would destroy thee.
I do not lie.²⁴

Stephano Trinculo, if you trouble him any more in's tale, by this   45
hand, I will supplant²⁵ some of your teeth.

Trinculo Why, I said nothing.

Stephano Mum, then, and no more. (*to Caliban*) Proceed.

Caliban I say, by sorcery he got this isle
From me, he got it. If thy greatness will   50
Revenge it on him, for I know thou dar'st,
But this thing²⁶ dare not.

Stephano That's most certain.

Caliban Thou shalt be lord of it, and I'll serve thee.

Stephano How now shall this be compassed?²⁷ Canst thou bring   55
me to the party?²⁸

Caliban Yea, yea, my lord, I'll yield him thee asleep,
Where thou may'st knock a nail into his head.

23 indeed, for sure
24 do not lie = am not lying
25 dispossess, uproot, remove*
26 Trinculo
27 planned, managed ("circled about," using a compass)
28 person, individual

	Ariel	Thou liest, thou canst not.
60	*Caliban*	What a pied ninny's[29] this? Thou scurvy patch![30]
		I do beseech thy greatness give him blows,
		And take his bottle from him. When that's gone
		He shall drink nought but brine, for I'll not show him
		Where the quick freshes[31] are.
65	*Stephano*	Trinculo, run into no further danger. Interrupt the
		monster one word further and by this hand, I'll turn my
		mercy out o' doors, and make a stockfish[32] of thee.
	Trinculo	Why, what did I? I did nothing. I'll go farther off.
	Stephano	Didst thou not say he lied?
70	*Ariel*	Thou liest.
	Stephano	Do I so? Take thou that. (*he hits Trinculo*) As[33] you like
		this, give me the lie another time.
	Trinculo	I did not give the lie. (*aside*) Out o' your wits, and
		hearing too? A pox o' your bottle. This can sack and
75		drinking do. (*openly*) A murrain[34] on your monster, and the
		devil take your fingers.
	Caliban	Ha, ha, ha!
	Stephano	Now forward with your tale. (*to Trinculo*) Prithee stand
		further off.
80	*Caliban*	Beat him enough. After a little time,
		I'll beat him too.
	Stephano	Stand farther. (*to Caliban*) Come, proceed.
	Caliban	Why, as I told thee, 'tis a custom with him

29 pied ninny = parti-colored fool (fools wore parti-colored costumes)
30 clown, booby
31 quick freshes = flowing streams / water sources
32 dried salt-cod, preliminarily softened by beating
33 to the extent that
34 plague

I' th' afternoon to sleep. There thou may'st brain him,
Having first seized his books. Or with a log   85
Batter his skull, or paunch[35] him with a stake,
Or cut his wezand[36] with thy knife. Remember
First to possess his books, for without them
He's but a sot,[37] as I am, nor hath not
One spirit to command. They all do hate him   90
As rootedly[38] as I. Burn but his books,
He has brave utensils[39] (for so he calls them)
Which when he has a house, he'll deck withal.
And that most deeply to consider, is
The beauty of his daughter. He himself   95
Calls her a nonpareil.[40] I never saw a woman
But only Sycorax my dam, and she,
But she as far surpasseth Sycorax
As great'st does least.

Stephano Is it so brave a lass?   100

Caliban Ay lord, she will become thy bed, I warrant,
And bring thee forth brave brood.[41]

Stephano Monster, I will kill this man. His daughter and I will be
king and queen, save our graces,[42] and Trinculo and thyself
shall be viceroys.[43] Dost thou like the plot,[44] Trinculo?   105

35 stab in the stomach
36 windpipe
37 blockhead
38 firmly, deeply
39 domestic apparatus (bowls, cups, etc.)
40 peerless, having no equal
41 offspring
42 honors
43 vice-kings
44 plan, scheme

Trinculo Excellent.

Stephano Give me thy hand, I am sorry I beat thee. But while thou liv'st, keep a good tongue in thy head.

Caliban Within this half hour will he be asleep,
110   Wilt thou destroy him then?

Stephano Ay, on mine honor.

Ariel   (*aside*) This will I tell my master.

Caliban Thou mak'st me merry: I am full of pleasure,
Let us be jocund.[45] Will you troll the catch[46]
115   You taught me but while-ere?[47]

Stephano At thy request, monster, I will do reason, any reason.[48]
Come on Trinculo, let us sing.

STEPHANO SINGS

Flout[49] 'em and scout[50] 'em,
and scout 'em and flout 'em,
120   Thought is free.

Caliban That's not the tune.

ARIEL PLAYS THE TUNE ON A TABOR[51] AND PIPE

Stephano What is this same?[52]

Trinculo This is the tune of our catch, played by the picture of Nobody.[53]

---

45 merry (DJAkund)
46 troll the catch = roundly sing the round-song
47 but while-ere = just a while ago
48 reason, any reason = what is reasonable, anything reasonable
49 mock, insult
50 deride, dismiss
51 small drum
52 repetition
53 a familiar figure – arms and legs, but no body – used on placards, store signs, etc.

Stephano If thou beest a man,[54] show thyself in thy likeness. If   125
    thou beest a devil, take't as thou list.[55]

Trinculo O forgive me my sins!

Stephano He that dies pays all debts. I defy thee. Mercy upon us.

Caliban Art thou afeard?

Stephano No monster, not I.   130

Caliban Be not afeard, the isle is full of noises,
    Sounds, and sweet airs,[56] that give delight and hurt not.
    Sometimes a thousand twangling[57] instruments
    Will hum about mine ears, and sometimes voices,
    That if I then had waked after long sleep,   135
    Will make me sleep again, and then in dreaming
    The clouds methought would open, and show riches
    Ready to drop upon me, that[58] when I waked
    I cried to dream again.

Stephano This will prove a brave kingdom to me, where I shall   140
    have my music for nothing.

Caliban When Prospero is destroyed.

Stephano That shall be by and by: I remember the story.[59]

Trinculo The sound is going away. Let's follow it, and after do
    our work.   145

Stephano Lead monster, we'll follow. I would I could see this
    taborer, he lays it on.[60]

Trinculo (*to Caliban*) Wilt come? I'll follow Stephano.

EXEUNT

54 a man = human
55 take't as thou list = do whatever you feel like doing
56 songs, music
57 the strumming of a stringed instrument
58 so that
59 recital of events
60 lays it on = really bangs away

SCENE 3

Another part of the Island

ENTER ALONSO, SEBASTIAN, ANTONIO, GONZALO,
ADRIAN, FRANCISCO, AND OTHERS

Gonzalo By'r Lakin,[1] I can go no further, sir,
  My old bones aches. Here's a maze[2] trod indeed
  Through forth-rights, and meanders.[3] By your patience,
  I needs must rest me.

Alonso   Old lord, I cannot blame thee,
5 Who am myself attached with[4] weariness
  To th' dulling of my spirits. Sit down, and rest.
  Even here I will put off[5] my hope, and keep it
  No longer for my flatterer.[6] He is drowned
  Whom thus we stray[7] to find, and the sea mocks
10 Our frustrate[8] search on land. Well, let him go.

Antonio (*aside to Sebastian*) I am right glad that he's so out of
  hope.
  Do not for[9] one repulse forgo[10] the purpose
  That you resolved to effect.[11]

Sebastian   (*aside to Antonio*) The next

---

1 by'r larkin = by our ladykin, watered-down form of "by our Lady" Mary
2 labyrinth
3 forth-rights, and meanders = straight/direct paths and turnings to and fro
4 attached with = fastened by
5 put off = dispose of
6 he who tries to persuade/flatter me that my son is still alive
7 wander
8 frustrated
9 because of
10 repulse forgo = rebuff/check neglect/pass over
11 accomplish, bring about

advantage[12]
Will we take throughly.

Antonio   (*aside to Sebastian*) Let it be tonight;
For now[13] they are oppressed with travel, they   15
Will not, nor cannot use such vigilance
As when they are fresh.

Sebastian   (*aside to Antonio*) I say tonight.
No more.

SOLEMN AND STRANGE MUSIC. PROSPERO ABOVE,[14]
INVISIBLE. ENTER SEVERAL STRANGE SHAPES, BRINGING
IN A BANQUET. THEY DANCE ABOUT IT WITH GENTLE
ACTIONS OF SALUTATION, AND INVITING THE KING,
&C., TO EAT, THEY DEPART

Alonso   What harmony is this? My good friends, hark.
Gonzalo   Marvelous sweet music.
Alonso   Give us kind keepers,[15] heavens! What were these?   20
Sebastian A living drollery.[16] Now I will believe
That there are unicorns. That in Arabia
There is one tree, the phoenix's[17] throne, one phoenix
At this hour reigning there.
Antonio   I'll believe both.
And what does else[18] want credit, come to me   25
And I'll be sworn 'tis true. Travelers ne'er did lie,

12 opportunity, chance
13 now that / when
14 i.e., on the "balcony," or small second stage, raised, center back
15 guardians
16 puppet show, comic play
17 legendary unique king of the birds, reproducing by burning itself and rising
   once more out of the ashes
18 what does else = whatever else

Though fools at home condemn them.

Gonzalo   If in Naples
I should report this now, would they believe me?
If I should say, I saw such islanders[19]

30   (For certes,[20] these are people of the island)
Who though they are of monstrous shape, yet note
Their manners are more gentle, kind[21] than of
Our human generation[22] you shall find
Many, nay almost any.

Prospero   (*aside*) Honest lord,

35   Thou hast said well. For some of you there present
Are worse than devils.

Alonso   I cannot too much muse[23]
Such shapes, such gesture, and such sound, expressing
(Although they want the use of tongue) a kind
Of excellent dumb discourse.[24]

Prospero   (*aside*) Praise in departing.[25]

Francisco   They vanished strangely.

40   *Sebastian*   No matter, since
They have left their viands[26] behind, for we have stomachs.
Will't please you taste of what is here?

Alonso   Not I.

Gonzalo   Faith sir, you need not fear. When we were boys

19 Folio: islands; all editors emend
20 certainly
21 more kind
22 species
23 wonder/marvel at
24 dumb discourse = mute/silent speech
25 praise in departing = wait until everything is done before you venture your
    praise (proverbial)
26 food, provisions

Who would believe that there were mountaineers,[27]
Dewlapped,[28] like bulls, whose throats had hanging at 'em   45
Wallets[29] of flesh? Or that there were such men
Whose heads stood[30] in their breasts? Which now we find
Each putter-out of five for one[31] will bring us
Good warrant of.

Alonso   I will stand to,[32] and feed,
Although my last, no matter, since I feel   50
The best is past. Brother, my lord the duke,
Stand to and do as we.

THUNDER AND LIGHTNING. ENTER ARIEL, LOOKING
LIKE A HARPY.[33] HE CLAPS HIS WINGS ON THE TABLE
AND, WITH A QUAINT DEVICE,[34] THE BANQUET VANISHES

Ariel   You are three[35] men of sin, whom Destiny –
That hath to[36] instrument this lower world
And what is in't – the never-surfeited sea   55
Hath caused to belch up you, and on[37] this island,
Where man doth not inhabit, you 'mongst men
Being most unfit to live. I have made you mad,

27 dwellers in mountain regions
28 having loose skin hanging from their throats, as cattle do (because of goiters?)
29 pouches
30 were located
31 broker-bettors on the survival of travelers headed abroad: it was five to one they'd survive
32 stand to = (1) get to work, (2) take the chance
33 mythical intensely ravenous monster with a woman's face and body and a bird's wings and claws
34 with a quaint device = by means of a clever/ingenious mechanism
35 Alonso, Antonio, and Sebastian
36 that hath to = which has as its
37 put/place you on

ALONSO, SEBASTIAN, &C., DRAW THEIR SWORDS

And even with such-like valor, men hang,[38] and drown
60   Their proper selves.[39] You fools! I and my fellows
Are ministers of fate, the elements[40]
Of whom[41] your swords are tempered[42] may as well[43]
Wound the loud winds, or with bemocked-at stabs
Kill the still[44]-closing waters, as diminish
65   One dowl[45] that's in my plume. My fellow ministers
Are like[46] invulnerable. If[47] you could hurt,
Your swords are now too massy[48] for your strengths,
And will not be uplifted. But remember
(For that's my business to[49] you) that you three
70   From Milan did supplant good Prospero,
Exposed unto the sea (which hath requit[50] it)
Him, and his innocent child. For which foul deed
The powers, delaying (not forgetting) have
Incensed the seas, and shores, yea, all the creatures
75   Against your peace. Thee of thy son, Alonso,
They have bereft,[51] and do pronounce by me

38 men hang = men are hanged (usually but not exclusively by other men)
39 their proper selves = themselves
40 basic natural substances
41 which
42 mixed, made
43 easily
44 forever
45 fiber of a feather
46 equally
47 and even if
48 weighty
49 with
50 (1) revenged, requited (shipwrecking them), (2) re-quit, abandoning
51 deprived

Lingering[52] perdition (worse than any death
Can be at once[53]) shall step by step attend
You, and your ways, whose wraths[54] to guard you from,
Which here, in this most desolate isle, else falls[55]   80
Upon your heads, is[56] nothing but hearts-sorrow,[57]
And a clear life ensuing.[58]

HE VANISHES IN THUNDER. THEN SOFT MUSIC,
AND THE SHAPES ENTER AGAIN. THEY DANCE,
WITH MOCKS AND MOWS, AND CARRY OUT THE TABLE

Prospero (*aside*) Bravely the figure[59] of this harpy hast thou
Performed, my Ariel. A grace it had, devouring.[60]
Of my instruction hast thou nothing bated[61]   85
In what thou hadst to say. So[62] with good life[63]
And observation strange,[64] my meaner[65] ministers
Their several kinds[66] have done. My high[67] charms work,
And these mine enemies are all knit up[68]

52 that lingering
53 at once = all at once
54 whose wraths = the anger of which powers (as per 6 lines earlier)
55 otherwise will fall
56 there is
57 remorse
58 clear life ensuing = pure life thereafter
59 image, representation
60 (1) in appearing to actually devour the food, as a harpy well might, (2) in
    making the food vanish
61 lessened, reduced
62 so too
63 (1) liveliness, energy, (2) naturalness
64 observation strange = attention of an exceptional order
65 lesser, inferior
66 several kinds = different/individual sorts of representations/roles
67 weighty, grave
68 knit up = tied, fastened

90 In their distractions.[69] They now are in my power,
And in these fits[70] I leave them, while I visit
Young Ferdinand (whom they suppose is drowned)
And his and mine loved darling.

EXIT PROSPERO ABOVE

Gonzalo I' the name of something holy, sir, why stand you
In this strange stare?[71]

95 *Alonso*   O, it is monstrous, monstrous!
Methought the billows spoke, and told me of it,
The winds did sing it to me, and the thunder
(That deep and dreadful organ-pipe) pronounced
The name of Prosper. It did bass my trespass.[72]

100 Therefore[73] my son i' th' ooze is bedded, and
I'll seek him deeper than e'er plummet[74] sounded,
And with him there lie mudded.

EXIT ALONSO

Sebastian   But[75] one fiend at a time,
I'll fight their legions o'er.[76]

Antonio   I'll be thy second.

EXEUNT SEBASTIAN AND ANTONIO

Gonzalo All three of them are desperate. Their great guilt,

69 (1) disorders, confusions, dissensions,★ (2) derangement, madness
70 paroxysms, crises
71 condition of staring amazement / horror
72 sing / sound the bass part to the song of my sin
73 that sin is the reason why
74 a depth-sounding / testing weight★
75 just, only
76 legions o'er = massive armies one after another

Like poison given to work a great time after,   105
Now 'gins to bite the spirits.[77] I do beseech you
(That are of suppler joints)[78] follow them swiftly,
And hinder them from what this ecstasy[79]
May now provoke[80] them to.
Adrian   Follow,[81] I pray you.

EXEUNT

77 bite the spirits = wound/affect/come home to their essential/basic
    natures/vital powers
78 suppler joints = more flexible limbs
79 frenzy
80 incite
81 follow after me

Act 4

SCENE I

The Island

ENTER PROSPERO, FERDINAND, AND MIRANDA

Prospero (*to Ferdinand*) If I have too austerely[1] punished you,
Your compensation[2] makes amends, for I
Have given you here a third[3] of mine own life,
Or that for which I live, who once again
I tender to thy hand. All thy vexations
Were but my trials of thy love, and thou
Hast strangely[4] stood the test. Here, afore Heaven,
I ratify[5] this my rich gift. O Ferdinand,
Do not smile at me that I boast her of,[6]
For thou shalt find she will outstrip[7] all praise

5

10

---

1 severely, harshly
2 recompense, requital
3 (?) himself, his daughter — and his wife?
4 wonderfully, exceptionally
5 confirm, validate
6 her of = of her
7 outrun, exceed

And make it halt[8] behind her.

Ferdinand   I do believe it
Against an oracle.[9]

Prospero   Then, as my gift and thine own acquisition
Worthily purchasd,[10] take my daughter. But
If thou dost break her virgin knot[11] before   15
All sanctimonious[12] ceremonies may
With full and holy rite be ministered,
No sweet aspersion[13] shall the heavens let fall
To make this contract grow, but barren hate,
Sour-eyed disdain,[14] and discord, shall bestrew   20
The union[15] of your bed with weeds[16] so loathly[17]
That you shall hate it both. Therefore take heed,
As Hymen's[18] lamps shall light you.

Ferdinand   As I hope
For quiet days, fair issue,[19] and long life
With such love as 'tis now, the[20] murkiest den,[21]   25
The most opportune[22] place, the strong'st suggestion[23]

---

8 limp
9 even in the face of an opposing prophetic judgment
10 obtained, gotten
11 virgin knot = hymen
12 sacred, holy
13 sprinkling/shower of grace
14 scorn, contempt
15 joining, coming together (sexual union, copulation)
16 i.e., instead of flowers
17 loathsome
18 the god of marriage (if the wedding torches burned clear and bright, it was
  considered a favorable omen)
19 children
20 not even the
21 murkiest den = darkest (and therefore most dangerous) hiding place
22 appropriate, suitable (oPORtune)
23 prompting toward evil

Our worser genius[24] can,[25] shall never melt[26]

Mine honor into lust, to take away

The edge[27] of that day's celebration,[28]

30 When[29] I shall think, or[30] Phoebus'[31] steeds are foundered,[32]

Or Night kept[33] chained below.

Prospero   Fairly spoke.[34]

Sit then, and talk with her, she is thine own.

What Ariel! My industrious servant Ariel!

ENTER ARIEL

Ariel   What would[35] my potent master? Here I am.

35 *Prospero* Thou, and thy meaner fellows, your last service

Did worthily perform. And I must use you

In such another trick. Go bring the rabble[36]

(O'er whom I give thee power) here to this place.

Incite them to quick motion, for I must[37]

40 Bestow[38] upon the eyes of this young couple

Some vanity[39] of mine art. It is my promise,

24 attendant spirit, guardian angel
25 can make
26 disintegrate (by the heat of lust)
27 keen passion, ardor
28 that day's celebration: their wedding
29 when in my impatience to make love to her
30 either
31 the sun god
32 are foundered = have gone lame
33 is being kept
34 fairly spoke = well said
35 wishes, desires
36 lower orders of spirits ("rank and file")
37 inCITE them TO quick MOtion FOR i MUST
38 confer, present, give, put*
39 slight/light display

And they expect it from me.

Ariel   Presently?

Prospero   Ay, with a twink.[40]

Ariel   Before you can say "Come," and "Go,"
And breathe twice, and cry "So, so,"   45
Each one, tripping[41] on his toe,
Will be here with mop[42] and mow.
Do you love me, master? No?[43]

Prospero   Dearly, my delicate Ariel. Do not approach
Till thou dost hear me call.

Ariel   Well.[44] I conceive.[45]   50

EXIT ARIEL

Prospero (*to Ferdinand*) Look thou be true. Do not give
dalliance[46]
Too much the rein.[47] The strongest oaths are straw
To th' fire i' the blood. Be more abstemious,[48]
Or else good night your vow!

Ferdinand   I warrant you, sir,
The white cold virgin snow upon my heart[49]   55
Abates the ardor of my liver.[50]

40 with a twink = in the twinkling of an eye
41 (1) nimbly, (2) dancing
42 grimace ("mops" and "mows" often occur in tandem)
43 don't you?
44 fine ("very well")
45 comprehend, understand
46 amorous caressing
47 too much the rein = too free a hand
48 abstinent (Ferdinand has apparently been observed by Prospero rather
    warmly engaged in dalliance)
49 the pure chastity of Miranda, leaning on his breast (?)
50 the liver was regarded as the site/center of passion

Prospero   Well.[51]

Now come, my Ariel! bring a corollary,[52]

Rather than want[53] a spirit. Appear, and pertly.[54]

(*to Ferdinand and Miranda*) No tongue. All eyes. Be silent.

SOFT MUSIC

ENTER IRIS[55]

60   *Iris*   Ceres,[56] most bounteous lady, thy rich leas[57]

Of wheat, rye, barley, vetches,[58] oats, and peas –

Thy turfy[59] mountains, where live nibbling sheep,

And flat meads[60] thatched with stover,[61] them to keep[62] –

Thy banks with pionèd[63] and twillèd brims[64]

65   Which spongy[65] April, at thy hest betrims,

To make cold[66] nymphs chaste crowns – and thy broom groves,[67]

Whose shadow the dismissèd[68] bachelor loves,

---

51 (spoken dryly?)

52 something over and above, a surplus

53 lack

54 (1) quickly, (2) visibly (since Ariel is so often invisible?)

55 virgin goddess of the rainbow, and messenger for the gods (pronounced like the flower, "iris")

56 goddess of agriculture (pronounced like "series")

57 open, arable land

58 beans used for forage

59 grassy

60 meadows

61 thatched with stover = covered with winter strawlike food for cattle

62 them to keep = to care for/maintain/feed said sheep

63 trenched, dug (PIEonED)

64 twillèd brims = borders/edges that are grained? striped?

65 damply soft: England in the spring is notoriously rainy ("April showers/bring May flowers")

66 sexually uninclined, frigid

67 shrubby small woods (and THY broom GROVES)

68 rejected

Being lass-lorn[69] – thy poll-clipt[70] vineyard,[71]
And thy sea-marge,[72] sterile and rocky-hard,
Where thou thyself dost air,[73] the queen o' the sky,   70
Whose[74] watery arch,[75] and messenger,[76] am I,
Bids thee leave these,[77] and with[78] her sovereign grace,[79]

JUNO'S[80] CHARIOT DESCENDS AND HANGS SUSPENDED
OVER THE STAGE

Here on this grass-plot, in this very place,
To come and sport. Her peacocks[81] fly amain.[82]
Approach, rich Ceres, her to entertain.[83]   75

ENTER CERES

Ceres (*to Iris*) Hail, many-colored messenger, that ne'er
    Dost disobey the wife of Jupiter.
    Who[84] with thy saffron[85] wings upon my flowers
    Diffusest[86] honey drops, refreshing showers,

69 abandoned, deserted
70 pruned at their tops (Folio: pole-clipped; English spelling was not
    standardized until long after Shakespeare's death)
71 vinYARD (the rhyme, in addition to the meter, requires this pronunciation)
72 sea-marge = sea-border, shore
73 take the air
74 the sky's
75 watery arch = moist arch: the rainbow (of which Iris is the goddess)
76 messenger of the sky/ the gods
77 i.e., all the locales just enumerated at some length
78 together with
79 elegance
80 wife of Jupiter and queen of the gods; patroness of women in general and
    marriage in particular
81 birds sacred to Juno; they draw her chariot
82 hard, at full speed
83 greet
84 you who
85 orange-red
86 spreads

80   And with each end of thy blue bow[87] dost crown
       My bosky[88] acres and my unshrubbed down,[89]
       Rich scarf[90] to my proud earth. Why hath thy queen
       Summoned me hither to this short-grassed[91] green?

Iris   A contract of true love to celebrate,
85   And some donation[92] freely to estate[93]
       On the blest lovers.

Ceres   Tell me heavenly bow,[94]
       If Venus or her son,[95] as thou dost know,
       Do now attend the queen? Since they did plot
       The means[96] that dusky Dis[97] my daughter got,[98]
90   Her and her blind boy's scandaled[99] company
       I have forsworn.[100]

Iris   Of her society[101]
       Be not afraid. I met her deity[102]
       Cutting[103] the clouds towards Paphos,[104] and her son

---

87 rainbow
88 bush- or shrub-filled
89 treeless elevated land, usually pasturage
90 the rainbow is like a scarf ("sash") to the earth below it
91 mowed/trimmed grass ("lawn")
92 gift
93 give, endow (verb)
94 BO, to rhyme with "know"
95 Cupid
96 method (an abduction)
97 Pluto, god of the underworld (Hades)
98 my daughter got = Prosperina (proSERpeeNA) obtained
99 scandalous, immoral
100 abandoned, renounced
101 companionship, company
102 godship
103 moving through by separating
104 city on the island of Cyprus

Dove-drawn[105] with her. Here thought they to have done[106]
Some wanton charm[107] upon this man and maid,   95
Whose vows are, that no bed-right[108] shall be paid
Till Hymen's torch be lighted, but in vain.
Mars's hot minion[109] is[110] returned again,
Her waspish-headed[111] son has broke his arrows,
Swears he will shoot no more, but play with sparrows,[112]   100
And be a boy right out.[113]

Ceres   Highest queen of state,[114]
Great Juno comes, I know her by her gait.[115]

ENTER JUNO

Juno   How does my bounteous sister? Go with me
To bless this twain, that they may prosperous[116] be,
And honored in their issue.   105

JUNO AND CERES SING

Juno   Honor, riches, marriage, blessing,
Long continuance, and increasing,
Hourly joys be still[117] upon you!

105 i.e., doves pull his chariot
106 worked, perpetrated
107 wanton charm = lewd/unchaste/naughty magical spell
108 bed-right = homage to Hymen: sexual intercourse
109 favorite, beloved: Venus, married to Vulcan but the mistress of and panting
      for Mars
110 has
111 petulant, irritable
112 Venus' birds
113 right out = completely, outright
114 of state = of high rank/greatness/magnificence
115 manner of walking ("carriage, bearing")
116 fortunate, thriving
117 always

Juno sings her blessings on you.

110 *Ceres*   Earth's increase, foison plenty,

Barns and garners[118] never empty.

Vines with clust'ring bunches growing,

Plants with goodly burden[119] bowing,[120]

Spring come to you at the farthest,[121]

115 In[122] the very end of harvest.[123]

Scarcity and want shall[124] shun you,

Ceres' blessing so[125] is on you.

Ferdinand This is a most majestic vision,[126] and

Harmonious charmingly.[127] May I be bold[128]

To think these spirits?

120 *Prospero*   Spirits, which by mine art

I have from their confines[129] called to enact

My present fancies.[130]

Ferdinand   Let me live here ever,

So rare a wondered[131] father, and a wise,

Makes this place Paradise.[132]

---

118 grain storehouses, granaries
119 loads
120 bending (BOing)
121 latest
122 at
123 in the fall: may there be no winter at all
124 must
125 thus
126 (1) sight, (2) dreamlike sight
127 fascinatingly, enchantingly
128 so bold as
129 regions, territories ("native regions")
130 present fancies = caprices/whims/fantasies of the moment
131 marvelous ("wondered-at")
132 makes THIS place PAraDISE

JUNO AND CERES WHISPER[133]

Prospero   (to Miranda)[134] Sweet now,
    silence.
    Juno and Ceres whisper seriously,   125
    There's something else to do. Hush, and be mute
    Or else our spell is marred.
Iris   You nymphs called Naiads,[135] of the windring[136]
    brooks,
    With your sedged crowns,[137] and ever-harmless looks,
    Leave your crisp[138] channels, and on this green land   130
    Answer your summons. Juno does command.
    Come temperate[139] nymphs, and help to celebrate
    A contract of true love. Be not too late.[140]

ENTER NYMPHS

    You sun-burned sickle-men,[141] of August weary,
    Come hither from the furrow,[142] and be merry,   135
    Make holiday. Your rye-straw hats put on,
    And these fresh nymphs encounter[143] every one

133 Folio adds "and send Iris on employment [an errand]." Yet she is almost
     immediately on stage and speaking, nor is there any indication that she has
     ever left.
134 i.e., Ferdinand having spoken, so too, now, might she
135 river nymphs (NEIGHadz)
136 (1) combination of "winding" and "wandering"? (if so, Shakespeare's
     creation), (2) typographical error?
137 sedged crowns = wreaths of river rushes / reeds
138 rippling
139 mild, moderate
140 slow
141 agricultural workers wielding reaping hooks
142 plowed-up trench
143 pair off with

In country footing.[144]

ENTER REAPERS, WHO JOIN WITH THE NYMPHS
IN A GRACEFUL DANCE, TOWARD THE END OF WHICH PROSPERO
STARTS SUDDENLY AND SPEAKS, AFTER WHICH, WITH A
STRANGE, HOLLOW, AND CONFUSED NOISE,
THE DANCERS RELUCTANTLY VANISH

Prospero   (*aside*) I had forgot that foul conspiracy
140   Of the beast Caliban, and his confederates
        Against my life. The minute of their plot
        Is almost come. (*to the Spirits*) Well done, avoid![145] No more.

EXEUNT SPIRITS

Ferdinand This is strange. Your father's in some passion
        That works[146] him strongly.
Miranda   Never till this day
145   Saw I him touched with[147] anger so distempered.[148]
Prospero   You do look, my son, in a moved sort,[149]
        As if you were dismayed.[150] Be cheerful sir,
        Our revels now are ended. These our actors
        (As I foretold you) were all spirits and
150   Are melted into air, into thin air,
        And like the baseless fabric[151] of this vision
        The cloud-capped towers, the gorgeous[152] palaces,

144 dancing
145 leave, go away
146 agitates
147 touched with = affected/struck by
148 disturbed, troubled, disordered
149 state, mood
150 appalled, overwhelmed
151 baseless fabric = groundless/without foundation-structure
152 magnificent, sumptuous

The solemn temples, the great globe itself,
Yea, all which[153] it inherit, shall dissolve
And like this insubstantial pageant faded[154]   155
Leave[155] not a rack[156] behind. We are such stuff
As dreams are made on,[157] and our little life
Is rounded[158] with a sleep. Sir, I am vexed,
Bear with my weakness, my old brain is troubled.
Be not disturbed with my infirmity.[159]   160
If you be pleased,[160] retire into my cell,
And there repose.[161] A turn or two I'll walk
To still my beating mind.

Ferdinand, Miranda   We wish[162] your peace.

EXEUNT

Prospero Come with a thought![163] (*to Ferdinand and Miranda*)
I thank thee. Ariel, come!

ENTER ARIEL

Ariel   Thy thoughts I cleave[164] to. What's thy pleasure?
Prospero   Spirit,   165

153 who
154 once faded
155 will leave
156 (1) puff of air, rush of wind, (2) cloud
157 of
158 rounded off, finished
159 weakness, feebleness
160 if you be pleased = please
161 rest
162 wish for
163 with a thought = with just the thought ("as swift as a thought")
164 attach myself, cling

We must prepare to meet with[165] Caliban.

Ariel   Ay my commander, when I presented[166] Ceres
I thought to have told thee of it, but I feared
Lest I might anger thee.

170 *Prospero* Say again, where didst thou leave these varlets?[167]

Ariel   I told you sir, they were red-hot with drinking,
So full of valor that they smote[168] the air
For breathing in their faces, beat the ground
For kissing of their feet, yet always bending[169]

175 Towards their project. Then I beat my tabor,
At which like unbacked[170] colts they pricked their ears,
Advanced their eyelids, lifted up their noses
As[171] they smelt music, so I charmed their ears
That[172] calf-like they my lowing[173] followed, through

180 Toothed briers, sharp furzes,[174] pricking goss,[175] and
thorns,[176]
Which entered their frail[177] shins. At last I left them
I' the filthy-mantled[178] pool beyond[179] your cell,

165 meet with = encounter, oppose
166 (1) acted the role of, (2) arrange/produced the masque/pageant
167 rogues, rascals, knaves
168 hit, struck, beat
169 turning, curving
170 untrained, not broken-in
171 as if
172 so that
173 mooing (LOWing)
174 spiny evergreen shrub
175 prickly shrub ("gorse")
176 toothed BRIers sharp FURzes PRICKing GOSS and THORNS
177 tender, weak
178 filthy-mantled = filth-covered/cloaked
179 on the far side of, farther away than

There dancing up to th' chins, that[180] the foul lake
O'erstunk[181] their feet.

Prospero   This was well done, my bird.[182]

Thy shape invisible retain thou still.   185

The trumpery[183] in my house, go bring it hither

For stale[184] to catch these thieves.

Ariel   I go, I go.

EXIT ARIEL

Prospero A devil, a born devil, on whose nature

Nurture[185] can never stick. On whom my pains,

Humanely[186] taken, all, all lost, quite lost,   190

And, as with age, his body uglier grows,

So his mind cankers.[187] I will plague[188] them all,

Even to roaring.

ENTER ARIEL, LOADED WITH GLISTENING APPAREL

Come, hang them on this line.[189]

PROSPERO AND ARIEL STAND TO THE SIDE, INVISIBLE
ENTER CALIBAN, STEPHANO, AND TRINCULO, WET

Caliban   Pray you tread softly, that the blind mole may not

180 so that
181 covered over with stink
182 youngster (affectionate: "chick")
183 worthless stuff, rubbish, trash
184 decoy, lure, bait
185 education, upbringing
186 compassionately, benevolently
187 is corrupted / infected / tarnished
188 torment, harass
189 (?) (1) a lime / linden tree★ (2) a clothesline

195　　　Hear a foot fall. We now are near his cell.

　　　Stephano　Monster, your fairy, which you say is a harmless fairy,
　　　　has done little better than played the Jack[190] with us.

　　　Trinculo　Monster, I do smell all horse piss, at which my nose is
　　　　in great indignation.[191]

200　*Stephano*　So is mine. Do you hear monster? If I should take a
　　　　displeasure against you – look you.[192]

　　　Trinculo　Thou wert[193] but a lost monster.

　　　Caliban　Good my lord, give me thy favor still,
　　　　Be patient, for the prize I'll bring thee to

205　　　Shall hoodwink[194] this mischance. Therefore speak softly;
　　　　All's hushed as midnight yet.

　　　Trinculo　Ay, but to lose our bottles in the pool![195]

　　　Stephano　There is not only disgrace and dishonor in that,
　　　　monster, but an infinite loss.

210　*Trinculo*　That's more to me than my wetting. Yet this is your
　　　　harmless fairy, monster.

　　　Stephano　I will fetch off[196] my bottle, though I be o'er ears[197]
　　　　for my labor.

　　　Caliban　Prithee, my king, be quiet. Seest thou here,

215　　　This is the mouth o' the cell. No noise, and enter.
　　　　Do that good mischief, which may make this island
　　　　Thine own forever, and I thy Caliban,
　　　　For aye thy foot-licker.

190　knave, scurvy fellow
191　(1) anger, (2) turning of the stomach
192　look you = take care, watch out
193　would be
194　cover up
195　deeper part of the bog/marsh
196　fetch off = rescue
197　o'er ears = over my ears in water

Stephano   Give me thy hand. I do begin to have bloody
  thoughts.   220
Trinculo   O King Stephano, O peer,[198] O worthy Stephano,
  look what a wardrobe here is for thee!
Caliban   Let it alone thou fool, it is but trash.
Trinculo   O, ho, monster! We know what belongs to[199] a
  frippery.[200] O King Stephano!   .   225
Stephano   Put off that gown,[201] Trinculo. By this hand, I'll have
  that gown.
Trinculo   Thy Grace shall have it.
Caliban   The dropsy[202] drown this fool, what do you mean
  To dote[203] thus on such luggage?[204] Let't alone[205]   230
  And do the murder first. If he awake,
  From toe to crown he'll fill our skins with pinches,
  Make us strange stuff.[206]
Stephano   Be you quiet, monster. Mistress line,[207] is not this my
  jerkin?[208] Now is the jerkin under the line.[209] Now jerkin,   235

---

198 nobleman (allusion to an old ballad, "Take Thy Old Cloak about Thee,"
    the 7th stanza of which begins "King Stephen was a worthy peer"; also
    referred to in *Othello* 2.3)
199 belongs to = is appropriate for
200 (1) fashionable/tawdry clothing, (2) old, cast-off clothing
201 loose-flowing upper garment worn by men
202 may the dropsy (a fatal disease that causes the body to accumulate water)
203 be so stupidly/foolishly fond of
204 terribly heavy baggage/encumbrances (perhaps, by extension, "nonsense,
    foolery"?)*
205 let't alone = leave it alone (Folio: let's alone; all editors emend)
206 make us strange stuff = turn us into different/unknown/alien material/
    textiles
207 the line/tree on which the clothes have been hung
208 close-fitting jacket worn by men
209 under the line = below the equator (crossing the equator was elaborately
    and merrily celebrated on ships)

III

you are like to lose your hair, and prove a bald jerkin.[210]

Trinculo   Do, do.[211] We steal by line and level,[212] an't like your
Grace.

Stephano   I thank thee for that jest. (*gives clothing*) Here's a
240   garment for't. Wit[213] shall not go unrewarded while I am
king of this country: "Steal by line and level" is an excellent
pass[214] of pate.[215] There's another garment for't.

Trinculo   Monster, come put some lime[216] upon your fingers,
and away with the rest.

245 *Caliban*   I will have none on't.[217] We shall lose our time,
And all be turned to barnacles, or to apes
With foreheads villainous[218] low.

Stephano   Monster, lay to[219] your fingers. Help to bear this away
where[220] my hogshead of wine is, or I'll turn you out of my
250   kingdom. Go to,[221] carry this.

Trinculo   And this.

Stephano   Ay, and this.

NOISE OF HUNTERS

210 the joke is obscure; clearly it is bawdy, referring either to syphilis (which
    causes hair to fall out) or to scurvy (which has the same effect), and that
    Stephano's movements and gestures illustrate the joke.
211 do, do = good, good ("way to go")
212 by line and level = with methodical accuracy (line = plumb line; level =
    tool determining horizontality)
213 (1) mental/intellectual capacity, (2) aptness of expression
214 (1) accomplishment, (2) fencing thrust
215 the head/brain/mind
216 bird lime: sticky substance used in bird-catching
217 of it
218 horribly, detestably
219 lay to = apply, set to work
220 to where
221 go to = come on

ENTER SPIRITS IN THE SHAPE OF HOUNDS, WHO HUNT
THE TRIO ABOUT, PROSPERO AND ARIEL SETTING THEM ON

Prospero Hey Mountain,[222] hey!

Ariel   Silver! There it goes, Silver!

Prospero Fury, Fury! There Tyrant, there! Hark, hark!   255

EXEUNT CALIBAN, STEPHANO, AND TRINCULO

Go, charge my goblins[223] that they[224] grind[225] their joints
With dry convulsions,[226] shorten[227] up their sinews
With agèd cramps,[228] and more pinch-spotted[229] make them
Than pard,[230] or cat o' mountain.[231]

Ariel   Hark, they roar.   260

Prospero Let them be hunted soundly.[232] At this hour
Lies at my mercy all mine enemies.
Shortly[233] shall all my labors end, and thou
Shalt have the air at freedom.[234] For a little
Follow, and do me service.   265

EXEUNT

222 mountain, silver, fury, tyrant = dog names
223 spirits, demons
224 they are to
225 torment ("grind into dust")
226 dry convulsions = severe/hard/stiff spasms
227 tighten
228 agèd cramps = cramps typical of old age
229 discolored with the marks of pinching
230 leopard, panther
231 cat o' mountain = mountain cat
232 thoroughly, to the full
233 soon
234 have the air at freedom = be able to fly through the air at your own free
    will

Act 5

SCENE I

The Island

ENTER PROSPERO IN HIS MAGIC ROBES, AND ARIEL

Prospero Now does my project gather to a head.[1]
   My charms crack[2] not, my spirits obey, and time
   Goes upright with his carriage.[3] How's the day?[4]
Ariel   On the sixth hour, at which time, my lord,
   You said our work should cease.
5 *Prospero*   I did[5] say so,
   When first I raised the tempest. Say my spirit,
   How fares the King, and 's[6] followers?
Ariel   Confined[7] together

---

1 gather to a head = acquire strength, come to a conclusion/culmination
2 collapse, come apart
3 goes upright with his carriage = carries his burden while walking erect/not
   stooping (the burden having become light)
4 how's the day = what time is it ("how far along is the day?")
5 did indeed
6 and 's = and his
7 enclosed, shut up

In the same fashion as you gave in charge,[8]
Just as you left them, all prisoners sir
In the line-grove which weather-fends[9] your cell.   10
They cannot budge till your release.[10] The King,
His brother, and yours, abide all three distracted,
And the remainder mourning[11] over them,
Brim full of sorrow, and dismay,[12] but chiefly
Him you termed sir, "the good old lord, Gonzalo."   15
His tears run down his beard like winter's drops
From eaves of reeds.[13] Your charm so strongly works 'em
That if you now beheld them, your affections
Would become tender.

Prospero   Dost thou think so, spirit?

Ariel   Mine would, sir, were I human.

Prospero   And mine shall.   20
Hast thou (which[14] art but air) a touch,[15] a feeling
Of their afflictions, and shall not myself,
One of their kind, that relish[16] all as sharply,
Passion[17] as they, be kindlier moved than thou art?
Though with their high wrongs I am struck to th' quick,[18]   25
Yet, with my nobler reason, 'gainst my fury

8 in charge = in trust/custody
9 weather-fends = shelters
10 your release = freeing/liberating them
11 sorrowing, lamenting
12 loss of resolution, inability to cope
13 eaves of reeds = roof edges on a thatched roof
14 who
15 (1) bit, (2) grasp
16 partake of, taste
17 am moved, feel (verb)
18 central/living core

Do I take part. The rarer action is
In virtue than[19] in vengeance. They, being penitent,
The sole drift[20] of my purpose doth extend
30   Not a frown further. Go, release them Ariel,
My charms I'll break, their senses I'll restore,
And they shall be themselves.

Ariel   I'll fetch them, sir.

EXIT ARIEL

Prospero Ye elves of hills, brooks, standing lakes, and groves,[21]
And ye that on the sands with printless foot[22]
35   Do chase the ebbing Neptune,[23] and do fly him[24]
When he comes back. You demi-puppets[25] that
By moonshine do the green sour ringlets[26] make,
Whereof the ewe not bites.[27] And you whose pastime
Is to make midnight mushrumps,[28] that rejoice
40   To hear the solemn curfew, by whose aid
(Weak masters[29] though ye be) I have bedimmed
The noontide sun, called forth the mutinous winds,
And 'twixt the green sea and the azured vault[30]

19 more than
20 impetus, progress (noun)
21 ye ELVES of HILLS brooks STANDing LAKES and GROVES
22 footstep
23 sea
24 fly him = flee/run away from the sea/Neptune
25 demi-puppets = half-sized supernatural beings ("fairies")
26 green sour ringlets = fairy rings (supposed to be from fairy dancing; actually
    caused by toadstools)
27 not bites = will not eat
28 mushrooms
29 instruments/tools/agents of magic
30 azured vault = blue sky

Set roaring war. To the dread rattling[31] thunder
Have I given fire,[32] and rifted Jove's stout oak   45
With his own bolt.[33] The strong-based[34] promontory
Have I made shake, and by the spurs[35] plucked up
The pine, and cedar. Graves at my command
Have waked their sleepers, op'd,[36] and let 'em forth
By my so[37] potent art. But this rough[38] magic   50
I here abjure.[39] And when I have required[40]
Some heavenly music (which even[41] now I do)
To work mine end upon their senses, that[42]
This airy charm is for, I'll break my staff,
Bury it certain[43] fathoms in the earth,   55
And deeper than did ever plummet sound
I'll drown my book.[44]

SOLEMN MUSIC

ENTER ARIEL, THEN ALONSO, WITH A FRANTIC GESTURE,[45]
ATTENDED BY GONZALO, THEN SEBASTIAN AND ANTONIO
IN LIKE MANNER, ATTENDED BY ADRIAN AND FRANCISCO.

31 making a succession of short, loud sounds
32 lightning
33 thunderbolt (bolt: a projectile / thick arrow)
34 strong-based = standing on a strong foundation-structure
35 principal roots
36 opened
37 thus, that
38 harsh, turbulent, violent
39 renounce, forswear, repudiate
40 commanded
41 just / right
42 those men that
43 deep ("permanent")
44 drown my book = throw it into the water, to sink
45 frantic gesture = wild / delirious bearing / deportment

THEY ALL ENTER THE CIRCLE THAT PROSPERO HAD MADE,[46]
AND THERE STAND ENCHANTED. PROSPERO OBSERVES THIS,
AND SPEAKS

A[47] solemn air, and the best comforter[48]
To an unsettled fancy,[49] cure thy brains,
60   Now useless, boil[50] within thy skull. There stand[51]
For you are spell-stopp'ed.[52]
Holy[53] Gonzalo, honorable man,
Mine eyes, ev'n sociable to the show[54] of thine,
Fall fellowly drops.[55] The charm dissolves apace,[56]
65   And as the morning steals upon[57] the night
(Melting the darkness) so their rising senses[58]
Begin to chase[59] the ignorant fumes[60] that mantle
Their clearer reason. O good Gonzalo
My true preserver, and a loyal sir[61]
70   To him thou follow'st, I will pay thy graces

46 drawing it with his magic staff
47 now let a
48 invigorating agent ("cordial": food or medicine that invigorates the heart
    and stimulates circulation)
49 unsettled fancy = disordered/disturbed imagination
50 and which boil
51 remain
52 spell-stopped = magically blocked/brought to a standstill
53 revered
54 ev'n sociable to the show = exactly susceptible/in accord with the look/
    appearance
55 fall fellowly drops = shed comradely tears
56 quickly
57 steals upon = stealthily/secretly attacks/overcomes
58 their rising senses = these men's ascending/increasing faculties
59 drive away
60 ignorant fumes = unknowing/uninformed vapors/exhalations
61 lord, gentleman

Home[62] both in word and deed. Most cruelly
Didst thou Alonso, use me and my daughter.
Thy brother was a furtherer[63] in the act:
Thou'rt pinch'd[64] for't now, Sebastian. Flesh and blood,
You, brother mine, that entertain[65] ambition,   75
Expelled remorse, and nature, whom,[66] with Sebastian
(Whose inward pinches therefore are most strong)
Would here have killed your king. I do forgive thee,
Unnatural though thou art. (*pauses*) Their understanding
Begins to swell, and the approaching tide   80
Will shortly fill the reasonable[67] shores
That now lie foul and muddy. Not one of them
That yet[68] looks on[69] me, or would know me. Ariel,
Fetch me the hat and rapier[70] in my cell,

EXIT ARIEL

I will discase[71] me, and myself present   85
As I was sometime Milan.[72] Quickly spirit,
Thou shalt ere long be free.

ENTER ARIEL. HE HELPS TO ATTIRE PROSPERO

62 pay thy graces = pay off your favors / goodwill
63 helper, supporter ("aider and abettor")
64 squeezed, nipped
65 harbor, are hospitable to
66 you whom
67 reasoning
68 that yet = as yet, still
69 at
70 small sword with a sharp point
71 undress
72 sometime Milan = in the past the Duke of Milan

Ariel   (*singing*)
> Where the bee sucks, there suck I,
>
> In a cowslip's bell[73] I lie,
>
90   There I couch[74] when owls do cry,
>
> On the bat's back I do fly
>
> After[75] summer merrily.[76]
>
> Merrily, merrily, shall I live now
>
> Under the blossom that hangs on the bough.

95   *Prospero* Why that's my dainty[77] Ariel. I shall miss thee,
> But yet thou shalt have freedom. (*attending to his garments*) So,
> so, so.
> (*to Ariel*) To[78] the king's ship, invisible as thou art,
> There shalt thou find the mariners asleep
> Under the hatches. The master and the boatswain
100   Being awake,[79] enforce[80] them to this place –
> And presently, I prithee.

Ariel   I drink the air before me, and return
> Or ere[81] your pulse twice beat.

EXIT ARIEL

Gonzalo All torment, trouble, wonder, and amazement
105   Inhabits here. Some heavenly power guide us
> Out of this fearful[82] country.

---

73 cowslip's bell = the bell-shaped primrose flower
74 lie down, sleep
75 chasing after, pursuing
76 MERriLY
77 delightful, excellent
78 go to
79 being awake = being awakened
80 drive, press, compel
81 or ere = before
82 terrible, awful

Prospero   Behold sir King,
The wrongèd Duke of Milan, Prospero.[83]
For more assurance[84] that a living prince
Does now speak to thee, I embrace thy body,[85]
And to thee and thy company I bid   110
A hearty welcome.

Alonso   Whe'er thou be'st he or no,
Or some enchanted trifle[86] to abuse[87] me
(As late I have been) I not know. Thy pulse
Beats as of[88] flesh and blood, and since I saw[89] thee,
Th' affliction[90] of my mind amends,[91] with which   115
I fear a madness held me. This must crave[92]
(And if this be[93] at all) a most strange story.
Thy dukedom[94] I resign, and do entreat
Thou pardon me my wrongs. But how should Prospero
Be living, and be here?

Prospero   (*to Gonzalo*) First, noble friend,   120
Let me embrace thine age,[95] whose[96] honor cannot
Be measured, or confined.

Gonzalo   Whether this be,

83 the WRONGed DUKE of MYlin PROSpeRO
84 certitude, pledge, guarantee
85 embrace thy body = put my arms around/clasp/hug you
86 fiction, fable
87 mistreat, injure, take advantage of
88 as of = like
89 have seen
90 misery, distress
91 is improved/repaired/healed
92 demand, ask, require
93 and if this be = if this is really happening
94 the awarding of the dukedom had been the tribute agreed upon by Antonio
95 old self/body
96 you whose

Or be not, I'll not swear.

Prospero   You do yet taste[97]

Some subtleties[98] o' the isle, that will not let you

125   Believe things certain. Welcome, my friends all,

(*aside to Sebastian and Antonio*) But you, my brace of lords,

were I so minded

I here could pluck[99] his Highness' frown upon you

And justify[100] you traitors. At this time

I will tell no tales.

Sebastian   The Divil[101] speaks in him.

Prospero   (*to Sebastian*)

No.

130   (*to Antonio*) For you, most wicked sir, whom to call brother

Would even infect[102] my mouth, I do forgive

Thy rankest fault[103] – all of them – and require[104]

My dukedom of thee, which perforce[105] I know

Thou must restore.

Alonso   If thou beest Prospero

135   Give us particulars of thy preservation,

How thou hast met[106] us here, whom three hours since

Were wracked upon this shore? Where I have lost

---

97 yet taste = still feel

98 deceptions, devices, tricks

99 draw

100 prove, condemn

101 devil (reconstructions of Shakespearean English sound very like modern Irish English)

102 stain, corrupt, sicken

103 rankest fault = largest/worst faults (fault: generically plural, though – today – singular)

104 demand

105 of necessity

106 found, come across, contacted

(How sharp the point of this remembrance is)
My dear son Ferdinand.

Prospero   I am woe[107] for't, sir.

Alonso   Irreparable is the loss, and patience   140
Says, it is past her cure.

Prospero   I rather think
You have not sought her help, of whose soft grace,
For the like loss, I have her sovereign[108] aid,
And rest myself content.

Alonso   You the like loss?

Prospero As great to me as late,[109] and supportable   145
To make the dear loss,[110] have I means much weaker[111]
Than you may call[112] to comfort you, for I
Have lost my daughter.

Alonso   A daughter?
O heavens, that they were living both in Naples,
The king and queen there! That[113] they were, I wish   150
Myself were mudded[114] in that oozy bed
Where my son lies. When did you lose your daughter?

Prospero In this last tempest.[115] I perceive these lords
At this encounter do so much admire[116]

107 sorry
108 supreme, superlative
109 as late = as it is recent
110 supportable to make the dear loss = to make the precious loss endurable/
       bearable/tolerable (SUPporTAble)
111 less powerful/strong
112 call on
113 to bring it about that
114 buried in the mud
115 (after this distinctly perfunctory response, Prospero changes the subject for
       some time)
116 wonder, marvel

155   That they devour[117] their reason, and scarce think
     Their eyes do offices of truth. Their words
     Are natural[118] breath. But howsoe'er you[119] have
     Been justled from your senses, know for certain
     That I am Prospero, and that very[120] duke
160   Which was thrust forth of Milan, who most strangely
     Upon this shore, where you were wracked, was landed
     To be the lord on't. No more yet of this,
     For 'tis a chronicle[121] of day by day,
     Not a relation[122] for a breakfast nor
165   Befitting this first meeting. Welcome, sir,[123]
     This cell's my court. Here have I few attendants
     And subjects none abroad.[124] Pray you, look in.
     My dukedom since you have given me again,
     I will requite you[125] with as good a thing,
170   At least bring forth a wonder to content[126] ye
     As much as me my dukedom.

PROSPERO OPENS THE CELL ENTRANCE, REVEALING
FERDINAND AND MIRANDA PLAYING CHESS

Miranda Sweet lord,[127] you play me false.[128]

---

117 destroy, consume, waste
118 instinctive (i.e., they are operating without being capable of thought – "on automatic pilot")
119 (?) he seems to be addressing all of the others, and not the King
120 same
121 history, story, account
122 narration
123 (Prospero here turns directly to the King)
124 at large, moving about
125 requite you = pay you back
126 satisfy, please, delight
127 husband
128 play me false = are cheating me

Ferdinand   No my dearest
  love,
  I would not for the world.
Miranda   Yes, for a score[129] of kingdoms you should
  wrangle — [130]
  And I would call it fair play.[131]
Alonso   If this prove   175
  A vision of the island,[132] one dear son
  Shall I twice lose.
Sebastian   A most high[133] miracle!
Ferdinand (*seeing Alonso*) Though the seas threaten they are
  merciful,
  I have cursed them without cause.

FERDINAND KNEELS TO ALONSO

Alonso   Now all the blessings
  Of a glad father compass thee about![134]   180
  Arise, and say how thou cam'st here.
Miranda   O wonder![135]
  How many goodly creatures are there here!
  How beauteous mankind is! O brave new world
  That has such people in't!
Prospero   'Tis new to thee.
Alonso   (*to Ferdinand*) What is this maid, with whom thou wast
  at play?   185

129 twenty ("a lot")
130 should wrangle = (1) would (2) ought to argue/debate
131 (i.e., she is so much in love that she would defend him, even then)
132 vision of the island = yet another of this island's illusions/fantasies
133 most high = immense
134 compass thee about = surround you
135 the complete prosodic line is RISE and SAY how THOU cam'st HERE o
     WONder

Your eld'st[136] acquaintance cannot be three hours.
Is she the goddess that hath severèd[137] us,
And brought us thus together?

Ferdinand   Sir, she is mortal,
But by immortal Providence, she's mine.

190   I chose her when I could not ask my father
For his advice, nor thought I had one.[138] She
Is daughter to this famous Duke of Milan,
Of whom, so often I have heard renown,[139]
But never saw before. Of[140] whom I have

195   Received a second life, and second father
This lady[141] makes him to me.

Alonso   I am hers.[142]
But O, how oddly will it sound that I
Must ask my child[143] forgiveness?

Prospero   There sir stop,
Let us not burden our remembrances
With a heaviness[144] that's gone.

200 *Gonzalo*   I have inly[145] wept,
Or should have spoke ere this. Look down you gods
And on this couple drop a blessèd crown,[146]

---

136 eldest = oldest, longest
137 parted, separated
138 i.e., a living father
139 the fame / distinction / honor
140 from
141 i.e., as his wife
142 I am hers = and I am now her father
143 not Ferdinand, but Miranda
144 grievance, sadness
145 internally
146 both a literal crown (Ferdinand being heir to a throne) and a figurative / celebrative crown

For it is you[147] that have chalked forth[148] the way[149]
Which brought us hither.

Alonso   I say amen, Gonzalo.

Gonzalo Was Milan thrust from Milan, that[150] his issue   205
Should become kings of Naples? O rejoice
Beyond a common joy, and set it down
With gold on lasting pillars.[151] In one voyage
Did Claribel her husband find at Tunis,
And Ferdinand her brother, found a wife   210
Where he himself was lost, Prospero[152] his dukedom
In a poor isle, and all of us[153] ourselves,
When no man was his own.[154]

Alonso   (*to Ferdinand and Miranda*) Give me your hands.
Let grief and sorrow still[155] embrace his heart ·   215
That doth not wish you joy.

Gonzalo   Be it so, amen.

ENTER ARIEL, WITH THE MASTER AND BOATSWAIN
AMAZEDLY FOLLOWING

O look sir, look sir, here is more of us!
I prophesied, if a gallows were[156] on land
This fellow could not drown. (*to Boatswain*) Now blasphemy,

---

147 the gods ("fate")
148 chalked forth = traced/marked out
149 path, road
150 so that
151 lasting pillars = permanent/enduring columns ("monuments")
152 Prospero found
153 all of us = all of us found
154 his own = (1) himself, (2) in charge/control of himself
155 always, forever
156 if a gallows were = if there were a gallows

220 That swear'st grace o'erboard,[157] not an oath on shore?

Hast thou no mouth by land? What is the news?

Boatswain The best news is, that we have safely found

Our King, and company. The next, our ship,

Which but three glasses since, we gave out[158] split,

225 Is tight and yare,[159] and[160] bravely rigged, as when

We first put out to sea.

Ariel (*aside to Prospero*) Sir, all this service

Have I done since I went.[161]

Prospero (*aside to Ariel*) My tricksy[162]

spirit!

Alonso These are not natural events, they strengthen[163]

From strange to stranger. (*to Boatswain*) Say, how came you

230 hither?

Boatswain If I did think, sir, I were well awake,

I'd strive to tell you. We were dead of sleep,[164]

And (how we know not) all clapped under hatches,[165]

Where, but even now, with strange and several noises

235 Of roaring, shrieking, howling, jingling chains,

And mo[166] diversity of sounds, all horrible,

We were awaked. Straightway, at liberty,

157 i.e., curses so immensely that God's grace is driven overboard / off the ship
158 gave out = declared, believed
159 tight and yare = watertight and ready / prepared
160 and as
161 have I done SINCE i WENT
162 fine, crafty, cunning
163 increase, intensify
164 of sleep = asleep
165 and HOW we KNOW not ALL clapped UNder HATches
166 more, additional

Where we, in all our trim,[167] freshly[168] beheld
Our royal, good, and gallant[169] ship, our master
Capering[170] to eye her. On a trice,[171] so please you,   240
Even[172] in a dream, were we divided from them,
And were brought moping[173] hither.

Ariel   (aside to Prospero) Was't well done?

Prospero (aside to Ariel) Bravely, my diligence,[174] thou shalt be
free.

Alonso   This is as strange a maze, as e'er men trod,[175]   245
And there is in this business more than nature
Was ever conduct of.[176] Some oracle[177]
Must rectify[178] our knowledge.

Prospero   Sir, my liege,[179]
Do not infest[180] your mind with beating[181] on
The strangeness of this business. At picked[182] leisure,   250
Which shall be shortly, single[183] I'll resolve[184] you

---

167 fully rigged and ready to sail
168 newly
169 fine, handsome, noble
170 dancing
171 on a trice = instantly ("in a single pull")
172 exactly as
173 bewildered
174 industrious/busy/hardworking one
175 have walked in
176 conduct of = a guide of/conductor in
177 mediating agency between the divine and the everyday worlds
178 set right, establish good order in ("correct")
179 superior-ranking lord
180 trouble
181 exercising your brain, hammering mentally
182 some chosen
183 solitary, alone
184 make clear/explain to

(Which to you shall seem probable)[185] of every[186]
These happened accidents.[187] Till when, be cheerful
And think of each thing well.[188] (*aside to Ariel*) Come hither
spirit,
255 Set Caliban and his companions free.
Untie the spell.

EXIT ARIEL

(*to Alonso*) How fares my gracious sir?
There are yet missing of[189] your company[190]
Some few odd lads[191] that you remember[192] not.

ENTER ARIEL, DRIVING IN CALIBAN, STEPHANO,
AND TRINCULO, WEARING THEIR STOLEN APPAREL

Stephano Every man shift for all the rest, and let no man take
260 care for himself, for all is but fortune. Coragio,[193] bully[194]
monster, coragio!
Trinculo If these be true spies[195] which I wear in my head,
here's a goodly sight.
Caliban O Setebos, these be brave spirits indeed.
265 How fine my master[196] is! I am afraid

185 demonstrable, plausible, reliable
186 every one of
187 happened accidents = occurring events
188 favorably ("think well of it all / everything")
189 from
190 retinue
191 few odd lads = small (1) remainder / surplus, (2) rather different / unusual
  varlets / servingmen / attendants
192 recall, bear in mind
193 have courage (Italian)
194 excellent, admirable
195 visual informers
196 Prospero

He will chastise[197] me.

Sebastian   Ha, ha!

What things[198] are these, my lord Antonio?

Will money buy 'em?

Antonio   Very like. One of them

Is a plain[199] fish, and no doubt marketable.

Prospero   Mark but the badges[200] of these men, my lords,   270

Then say if they be true.[201] This misshapen[202] knave,

His mother was a witch, and one so strong

That[203] could control the moon, make flows and ebbs,

And deal in her command,[204] without her[205] power.

These three have robbed me, and this demi-devil   275

(For he's a bastard one) had plotted with them

To take my life. Two of these fellows you

Must know[206] and own,[207] this thing of darkness I

Acknowledge mine.[208]

Caliban   I shall be pinched to death.

Alonso   Is not this Stephano, my drunken butler?   280

Sebastian   He is drunk now, where had he[209] wine?

197 discipline, punish
198 creatures
199 obvious, unmistakable
200 distinguishing signs (i.e., the stolen clothes)
201 faithful, loyal, trustworthy
202 deformed, monstrous
203 that she
204 deal in her command = share in the moon's authority/rule power
205 without her = outside/beyond the moon's
206 recognize, identify
207 acknowledge
208 is mine
209 had he = did he get/obtain

Alonso   And Trinculo is reeling ripe.[210] Where should[211] they
　　　　Find this grand[212] liquor that hath gilded[213] 'em?
　　　　How cam'st thou in this pickle?[214]

285 *Trinculo*   I have been in such a pickle[215] since I saw you last
　　　　that[216] I fear me will never out of my bones. I shall not fear
　　　　fly-blowing.[217]

Sebastian   Why, how now Stephano?

Stephano   O touch me not, I am not Stephano, but a cramp.[218]

290 *Prospero*   You'd be[219] king o' the isle, sirrah?[220]

Stephano   I should[221] have been a sore[222] one, then.[223]

Alonso   (*looking at Caliban*) This is a strange thing[224] as e'er I
　　　　looked on.

Prospero   He is as disproportioned[225] in his manners
　　　　As in his shape. (*to Caliban*) Go sirrah, to my cell,
295 　　　　Take with you your companions. As[226] you look[227]

---

210 reeling ripe = fully drunk ("fully advanced to the stage of reeling")
211 could
212 fine, imposing
213 brilliantly flushed their faces
214 sorry condition, disagreeable predicament
215 salt/brine used to pickle food (a pun)
216 the pickling
217 i.e., he is so well pickled that flies will not alight on him
218 caused by too much alcohol? or (since Stephano has just made a very active
　　entrance) by Prospero's magic?
219 you'd be = you wished to be
220 term of address, when used for men, expressing control/contempt; also
　　used, less severely, with children
221 would/must
222 painful, grievous
223 had I been/become king
224 a strange thing = as strange a thing
225 out of proportion/balance, inconsistent
226 insofar as
227 expect, look for

To have my pardon, trim it handsomely.[228]

Caliban   Ay that I will. And I'll be wise hereafter,
And seek for grace.[229] What a thrice-double[230] ass
Was I to take this drunkard for a god,
And worship this dull fool!

Prospero   Go to, away.   300

Alonso   (to Stephano and Trinculo) Hence, and bestow your
luggage where you found it.

Sebastian Or stole it, rather.

EXEUNT CALIBAN, STEPHANO, AND TRINCULO

Prospero   Sir, I invite your Highness, and your train[231]
To my poor cell, where you shall take your rest
For this one night, which part of it[232] I'll waste[233]   305
With such discourse as, I not doubt, shall make it
Go quick away, the story of my life
And the particular accidents,[234] gone by[235]
Since I came to this isle. And in the morn
I'll bring you to your ship, and so to Naples,   310
Where I have hope to see the nuptial
Of these our dear-belov'd solemnized,[236]
And thence retire me to my Milan, where
Every third thought shall be my grave.

228 trim it handsomely = put the cell in very good condition
229 favor, goodwill, forgiveness
230 triple double
231 attendants
232 which part of it = which in part
233 consume, spend
234 particular accidents = (1) peculiar/singular, (2) personal/private events/
      happenings
235 gone by = which have passed
236 soLEMniZED

Alonso   I long
315   To hear the story of your life, which must
          Take[237] the ear strangely.
Prospero   I'll deliver all,
          And promise you calm seas, auspicious gales,[238]
          And sail,[239] so expeditious, that shall[240] catch
          Your royal fleet far off.[241] (*aside to Ariel*) My Ariel, chick,
320   That is thy charge. Then to the elements
          Be free, and fare thou well! (*to his guests*) Please you draw
          near.

EXEUNT

237 grasp, grip, engage, affect ("take hold of ")
238 auspicious gales = favorable but brisk winds
239 sailing
240 you will
241 far off = now a day's sail away

Epilogue

Now my charms[1] are all o'erthrown,[2]
And what strength I have's mine own.[3]
Which is most faint.[4] Now 'tis true[5]
I must be here confined[6] by you,
Or sent to Naples.[7] Let me not   5
Since I have my dukedom got,
And pardoned the deceiver, dwell
In this bare[8] island[9] by your spell,[10]
But release me from my bands[11]

1 (1) magic spells, (2) graces, fascinating qualities
2 demolished, overcome
3 mine own = (1) as character in the play, (2) as actor playing (and still in
   costume as) a character in the play
4 feeble, weak
5 (1) clear, settled, sure, (2) the truth/reality/accurate, (3) proper, right,
   legitimate
6 (1) restricted, (2) banished (as he was for so many years confined/banished
   on the island)
7 i.e., very, very far from London, where the theater is
8 (1) desolate, (2) defenseless, (3) needy, poor, (4) without artistic merit,
   meager, rude
9 (1) the stage, (2) the play's island
10 magic power, since you are the all-powerful theater audience
11 bonds, restrictions

10 With the help of your good hands.[12]
    Gentle[13] breath[14] of yours, my sails[15]
    Must fill,[16] or else my project fails,
    Which was to please. Now I want[17]
    Spirits[18] to enforce,[19] art[20] to enchant,[21]
15 And my ending[22] is despair,
    Unless I be relieved[23] by prayer[24]
    Which pierces[25] so that it assaults[26]
    Mercy itself, and frees[27] all faults.[28]
    As[29] you from crimes[30] would[31] pardoned be,
20 Let your indulgence[32] set me free.[33]

EXIT

12 (i.e., by applause: noise was also thought to break magic spells)
13 noble, kind
14 words, sounds of approval
15 (1) as on a boat, (2) as the wings of a poet/playwright, (3) as metaphors of prosperity/success ("to live at low sail" = to live humbly)
16 swell (as in the various senses of "sails," in the note just above)
17 (1) lack, (2) desire
18 (1) sprites, as in the play, (2) personal characteristics/powers, (3) courage
19 (1) drive by force, overcome, compel, (2) intensify/strengthen (the audience)
20 (1) learning, as a scholar/magician, (2) skill, as a poet/playwright, (3) cunning, stratagems
21 (1) magically bewitch, (2) fool, delude, (3) please, delight
22 (pun on "ending" as [1] fate and [2] end of a play/narrative)
23 (1) rescued, (2) given sustenance, (3) lifted up, encouraged
24 this prayer of mine, to you as my heavenly authority
25 penetrates, thrusts through
26 attacks, persuades, convinces
27 relieves me/my play from
28 (1) sins, (2) dramatic errors
29 just as
30 offenses, sins
31 wish to
32 (1) grace, over-lenient treatment, (2) ecclesiastical remission from the consequences of sin, as in Catholic practice
33 of my confinement/banishment

The *Tempest* led off the First Folio in 1623, seven years after the death of Shakespeare. Edward Dowden, an Anglo-Irish critic of the later nineteenth century, first referred to Shakespeare's final group of plays as the Late Romances. Though I regard Dowden's suggestion as unfortunate, it has become universal and no longer can be overturned. In the First Folio, *The Tempest* clearly is regarded by Shakespeare's co-workers as a comedy, and I believe that we should think of it, and of *The Winter's Tale,* as tragi-comedies.

Shakespeare exorcised Christopher Marlowe through a long process that went on from about 1589 to 1595. With the composition of *Romeo and Juliet, Richard II, King John, A Midsummer Night's Dream,* and *Love's Labor's Lost,* in 1595–97, the ghost of Marlowe became amenable to summoning or dismissal at Shakespeare's own will. In 1597, Shylock and Falstaff were created, both of them beyond the horizons of Marlowe's art. It is delightful to see Shakespeare deliberately parody Marlowe in *Richard II,* and rather touching to encounter the sadness of Marlowe's murder by Walsingham's Elizabethan CIA, covertly in *As You Like It.* Echoes of Marlowe are scarce after that as Shakespeare moves into the phase of the great tragedies of 1601 to 1607. Yet Shakespeare invents new modes of allusion, which we scarcely know as yet how to comprehend. *The Tempest* is Shakespeare's belated answer to Marlowe's *Doctor Faustus* and Prospero is the Anti-Faust, even though his name slyly is the Italian version of the Latin Faustus, "the favored one." Faustus was the cognomen that Simon Magus, reviled by Christianity as the originator of the Gnostic heresy, took when he arrived in Rome, where he perished, according to Christian sources, in a rather unlikely levitation contest with Saint Peter. Marlowe's Faustus acquires Mephistopheles as his magical familiar, but Shakespeare's Prospero employs Ariel instead, and so has made no bargain with the darker powers. Shakespeare's magus is a white magician of the Hermetist kind, possibly on the model of Giordano Bruno or of Doctor John Dee. Yet Prospero surpasses all precursors in his triumphant mastery over nature and his fellow human beings. Though such central Shakespearean figures as Hamlet, Falstaff, Iago, and Cleopatra have engendered a varied progeny in later writers, Prospero remains a largely unused resource. He is so uncanny that we have not yet caught up with him.

The Tempest is not a mystery play, offering a secret insight into human finalities; act 5 of *Hamlet* is closer to that. Perhaps *The Tempest* does turn ironically upon Shakespeare's conscious farewell to his dramatic art, but such an irony or allegory does not enhance the play's meanings. I sometimes think *The Tempest* was the first significant drama in which not much happens, beyond its protagonist's abandonment of his scheme of justified revenge precisely when he has all his enemies in his power. Most explanations of Prospero's refusal to take revenge reduce to the formulaic observation: "That's the way things turn out in Shakespeare's late romances." Let us reopen the question: why does Prospero not gratify himself by fulfilling his revenge?

The originality of representation in *The Tempest* embraces only Prospero, the supernatural Ariel, compounded of fire and air, and the preternatural Caliban, compounded of earth and water. Unlike *The Winter's Tale, The Tempest* contrives to be a comedy of the marvelous without ever being outrageous; the Shakespearean exuberance expresses itself here by cheerfully discarding any semblance of a plot, except ironically that of Caliban and his drunk companions against Prospero's life.

Prospero, who is almost always sympathetic as Miranda's father, is dubiously fair to Ariel, and almost too grimly censorious towards the wretched Caliban. His peculiar severity towards Ferdinand also darkens him. But this split, between loving father and puritanical Hermetist, helps make Prospero truly interesting. He does not move our imagination as Ariel does, and Ariel, a kind of revised Puck, is less original a representation than Caliban is. Caliban does not run off with the play, as Barnardine does in *Measure for Measure,* but he makes us wonder how much humanity Prospero has sacrificed in exchange for Hermetic knowledge and wisdom.

Caliban is uncanny to us, in precisely Freud's sense of "the uncanny." Something long estranged from us, yet still familiar, returns from repression in Caliban. We can be repelled by Caliban's degradation and by his deformity, but like Prospero we have to acknowledge that Caliban is somehow ours, not to be repudiated. It is not clear to me whether Caliban is meant to be wholly human, as there is something amphibian about him, and his mother, Sycorax, like the weird sisters in *Macbeth,* has her preternatural aspects. What is certain is that Caliban has aesthetic dignity, and that the play is not wholly Prospero's only because of him. You could replace Ariel by various assistant sprites (though not without loss), but you would not have *The Tempest* if you removed Caliban.

Why Shakespeare called the play *The Tempest* I cannot understand. Perhaps he should have called it *Prospero* or even *Prospero and Caliban*. Though the "names of the actors" describes Caliban as a "savage and deformed slave," I have never known any reader or theatergoer who could regard that as an adequate account of what may be Shakespeare's most deeply troubling single representation after Shylock. Robert Browning's Caliban, in the great monologue "Caliban upon Setebos," seems to me the most remarkable interpretation yet ventured, surpassing all overt literary criticism, and so I will employ it here as an aid, while yielding to all those who would caution me that Browning's Caliban is not Shakespeare's. Yes, but whose Caliban is?

Prospero forgives his enemies (and evidently will pardon Caliban) because he achieves a complex stance that hovers between the disinterestedness of the Hamlet of act 5 and a kind of Hermetic detachment from his own powers, perhaps because he sees that even those are dominated by a temporal ebb and flow. But there is also a subtle sense in which Prospero has been deeply wounded by his failure to raise up a higher Caliban, even as Caliban is palpably hurt (in many senses) by Prospero. Their relations, throughout the play, are not less than dreadful and wound us also, as they seem to have wounded Browning, judging by his Caliban's meditation:

Himself peeped late, eyed Prospero at his books
Careless and lofty, lord now of the isle:

Vexed, 'stiched a book of broad leaves, arrow-shaped,
Wrote thereon, he knows what, prodigious words;
Has peeled a wand and called it by a name;
Weareth at whiles for an enchanter's robe
The eyed skin of a supple oncelot;
And hath an ounce sleeker than youngling mole,
A four-legged serpent he makes cower and couch,
Now snarl, now hold its breath and mind his eye,
And saith she is Miranda and my wife:
'Keeps for his Ariel a tall pouch-bill crane
He bids go wade for fish and straight disgorge;
Also a sea-beast, lumpish, which he snared,
Blinded the eyes of, and brought somewhat tame,
And split its toe-webs, and now pens the drudge
In a hole o' the rock and calls him Caliban;
A bitter heart that bides its time and bites.
'Plays thus at being Prosper in a way,
Taketh his mirth with make-believes: so He. (ll. 150–169)

That lumpish sea-beast, "a bitter heart that bides its time and bites," is the tortured plaything of a sick child, embittered by having been cast out by a foster father. Prospero's failed adoption of Caliban festers in the magus throughout the play. Like Emerson, who dismissed the Crucifixion as a Great Defeat, and insisted: "We demand Victory," Prospero also declines to accept defeat. These peculiar days, Prospero is regarded as a vicious Colonialist by the academic coven that calls itself Post-Colonialist. My own response would be he is in many ways a would-be father embittered by a badly failed adoption. When I stood up to depart from the New York Public Theater, soon after George C. Wolfe's production of *The Tempest* began, I recall muttering to myself that *The Tempest* was being converted into theater for ideologues. Wolfe gave us Caliban as an heroic West-Indian Freedom Fighter, and Ariel as another heroic rebel who hated Prospero. What Shakespeare actually had composed did not matter to Wolfe, or the New York reviewers, or the audience.

As a slave, Shakespeare's actual Caliban is rhetorically defiant, but his curses are his only weapon. Since he has not inherited his mother's powers, Caliban's curses are in vain, and yet they have the capacity to provoke Prospero and Miranda, as in the first scene where the three appear together:

Prospero   Come on,
We'll visit Caliban, my slave, who never
Yields us kind answer.

Miranda   'Tis a villain, sir,
I do not love to look on.

Prospero   But as 'tis
We cannot miss him. He does make our fire,
Fetch in our wood, and serves in offices
That profit us. What ho! slave! Caliban!
Thou earth, thou! Speak.

Caliban   (*within*) There's wood enough
within.

Prospero Come forth, I say, there's other business for thee.
Come thou tortoise! When?

ENTER ARIEL AS A WATER NYMPH

(*to Ariel*) Fine apparition. My quaint Ariel,
Hark in thine ear.

PROSPERO WHISPERS IN ARIEL'S EAR

Ariel   My lord, it shall be done.

EXIT ARIEL

Prospero (*to Caliban*) Thou poisonous slave, got by the Devil
   himself
   Upon thy wicked dam, come forth!

ENTER CALIBAN

Caliban As wicked dew, as e'er my mother brushed
   With raven's feather from unwholesome fen
   Drop on you both! A south-west blow on ye,
   And blister you all o'er!
Prospero For this be sure, tonight thou shalt have cramps,
   Side-stitches that shall pen thy breath up, urchins
   Shall for that vast of night that they may work
   All exercise on thee. Thou shalt be pinched
   As thick as honeycomb, each pinch more stinging
   Than bees that made 'em.
Caliban   I must eat my dinner.
   This island's mine by Sycorax my mother,
   Which thou tak'st from me. When thou cam'st first
   Thou strok'st me, and made much of me. Wouldst give me
   Water with berries in't. And teach me how
   To name the bigger light, and how the less
   That burn by day and night. And then I loved thee,
   And showed thee all the qualities o' th' isle,
   The fresh springs, brine-pits, barren place, and fertile.
   Cursed be I that did so! All the charms
   Of Sycorax, toads, beetles, bats, light on you!
   For I am all the subjects that you have,

Which first was mine own king. And here you sty me
In this hard rock, whiles you do keep from me
The rest o' th' island.

Prospero　　　　　　　Thou most lying slave,
Whom stripes may move, not kindness! I have used thee,
Filth as thou art, with humane care, and lodged thee
In mine own cell, till thou didst seek to violate
The honor of my child.

Caliban　Oh ho, oh ho, would't had been done!
Thou didst prevent me, I had peopled else
This isle with Calibans.

Miranda　　　　　　　Abhorrèd slave,
Which any print of goodness wilt not take,
Being capable of all ill. I pitied thee,
Took pains to make thee speak, taught thee each hour
One thing or other. When thou didst not, savage,
Know thine own meaning, but wouldst gabble like
A thing most brutish, I endowed thy purposes
With words that made them known. But thy vile race,
Though thou didst learn, had that in't which good natures
Could not abide to be with. Therefore wast thou
Deservedly confined into this rock, who hadst
Deserved more than a prison.

Caliban　You taught me language, and my profit on't
Is, I know how to curse. The red plague rid you
For learning me your language!

Prospero　　　　　　　　　Hag-seed, hence!
Fetch us in fuel, and be quick thou 'rt best,
To answer other business. Shrug'st thou, malice?
If thou neglect'st, or dost unwillingly
What I command, I'll rack thee with old cramps,

> Fill all thy bones with aches, make thee roar,
> That beasts shall tremble at thy din.
> *Caliban*   No, pray thee.
>   (*aside*) I must obey. His art is of such power,
>   It would control my dam's god Setebos,
>   And make a vassal of him.
> *Prospero*   So slave, hence! (1.2.307–375)

Is it, as some would say, that our resentment of Prospero and Miranda here and our sympathy (to a degree) with Caliban, are as irrelevant as a preference for Shylock over Portia? I do not think so, since Shylock is a grotesque bogeyman though also a troublingly original representation, while Caliban, though grotesque, is also immensely original. You can New Historicize Caliban if you wish, but a discourse on Caliban and the Bermudas Trade is about as helpful as a Neo-Marxist analysis of Falstaff and Surplus Value, or a Lacanian-Feminist exegesis of the difference between Rosalind and Celia. Caliban's peculiar balance of character and personality is as unique as Falstaff's and Rosalind's, though far more difficult to describe. But Prospero's balance also yields reluctantly to our descriptions, as if more than his white magic is beyond us. Prospero never loses his anger or sense of outrage in regard to Caliban, and surely some guilt attaches to the magus, who sought to make Caliban into what he could not become, and then went on punishing Caliban merely for being himself. Caliban is an inhabitant of his own island and its nature, and not at all a candidate for Hermetic transformations. He can be controlled and chastised by Prospero's magical art, but he remains recalcitrant, and holds on to the strange dignity of being Caliban, although endlessly insulted by everyone who speaks to him in the play.

More than victimage and its ravages is involved when we sympathize with Caliban. What Freud called Family Romances is the context that holds together Prospero, Miranda, and Caliban. The attempted rape is ignored by New Historicists, Feminists, Marxists, Post-Colonialists, and the other components of what I have dubbed The School of Resentment, but it must be meditated upon even as we remain concerned with the pathos of Caliban. Prospero has his Yahweh-like aspects, and indeed even admits he has raised the dead. Himself a great usurper of preternatural powers, Prospero is outraged as much by Caliban's would-be yielding to what Freud called the Drive, as he is by the foster child's betrayal of familial constraints. I have quoted this first confrontation between Prospero and Miranda with Caliban in the play at such length because it seems to me the heart of darkness in *The Tempest*. Time is Prospero's only authentic antagonist in the drama, and the collapse of the scheme of adoption threatens the ordering of time by the magus. Yet even the marring of Prospero's project of raising up Caliban cannot deprive the creature of his aesthetic dignity.

Alas, Caliban's dignity vanishes in the presence of the jester Trinculo and the drunken Stephano, with whom Caliban attempts to replace Prospero as master. The immense puzzle of Shakespeare's vision of Caliban is enhanced when the slave's most beautiful speech comes in the grotesque context of his seeking to soothe the fears of Trinculo and Stephano which are caused by the music of the invisible Ariel:

Be not afeard, the isle is full of noises,
Sounds, and sweet airs, that give delight and hurt not.
Sometimes a thousand twangling instruments

Will hum about mine ears, and sometimes voices,
That if I then had waked after long sleep,
Will make me sleep again, and then in dreaming
The clouds methought would open, and show riches
Ready to drop upon me, that when I waked
I cried to dream again. (3.2.135–143)

This exquisite pathos is Caliban's finest moment, and exposes the sensibility that Prospero presumably hoped to develop, before Caliban's attempted rape of Miranda. The bitterest lines in the play come in Prospero's Yahweh-like reflections upon his fallen creature:

A devil, a born devil, on whose nature
Nurture can never stick. On whom my pains,
Humanely taken, all, all lost, quite lost,
And, as with age, his body uglier grows,
So his mind cankers. I will plague them all,
Even to roaring. (4.1.88–93)

This could be Milton's God, Schoolmaster of Souls, fulminating at the opening of *Paradise Lost,* book 3. True, Prospero turns to the rarer action of forgiveness and promises Caliban he yet will receive pardon and Caliban resolves to "seek for grace." Yet Shakespeare was uninterested in defining that grace; he does not even tell us if Caliban will remain alone on the island in freedom, or whether he is to accompany Prospero to Milan, a weird prospect for the son of Sycorax, and yet by no means an unlikely one. All that Prospero foresees for himself in Milan is a retirement "where / Every third thought shall be my grave." We want Caliban to be left behind in what is, after all, his own place, but

Shakespeare neither indulges nor denies our desires. If Prospero is at last a kind of benign Iago (an impossible oxymoron), then Caliban's recalcitrances finally look like an idiosyncratic rebellion of actor against playwright, creature against demiurge. A warm monster is dramatically more sympathetic than a cold magus, but that simplistic difference does not explain away the enigma of Caliban. I suspect that Prospero forgives his enemies because he understands, better than we can, the mystery of time. His magic reduces to what Nietzsche called the will's revenge against time, and against time's "it was." Caliban, who need not fear time, and who hates Prospero's books of magic, perhaps represents finally time's revenge against all those who conjure with books.

FURTHER READING

This is not a bibliography but a selective set of starting places.

Texts

Hinman, Charlton. *The First Folio of Shakespeare*. 2d ed. Introduction by Peter W. M. Blayney. New York: W. W. Norton, 1996.

Language

Dobson, E. J. *English Pronunciation, 1500–1700*. 2d ed. Oxford: Oxford University Press, 1968.

Houston, John Porter. *The Rhetoric of Poetry in the Renaissance and Seventeenth Century*. Baton Rouge: Louisiana State University Press, 1983.

————. *Shakespearean Sentences: A Study in Style and Syntax*. Baton Rouge: Louisiana State University Press, 1988.

Kermode, Frank. *Shakespeare's Language*. New York: Farrar, Straus and Giroux, 2000.

Kökeritz, Helge. *Shakespeare's Pronunciation*. New Haven: Yale University Press, 1953.

Lanham, Richard A. *The Motives of Eloquence: Literary Rhetoric in the Renaissance*. New Haven and London: Yale University Press, 1976.

The Oxford English Dictionary: Second Edition on CD-ROM, version 3.0. New York: Oxford University Press, 2002.

Raffel, Burton. *From Stress to Stress: An Autobiography of English Prosody.* Hamden, Conn.: Archon Books, 1992.

Ronberg, Gert. *A Way with Words: The Language of English Renaissance Literature.* London: Arnold, 1992.

Trousdale, Marion. *Shakespeare and the Rhetoricians.* Chapel Hill: University of North Carolina Press, 1982.

Culture

Bindoff, S. T. *Tudor England.* Baltimore: Penguin, 1950.

Bradbrook, M. C. *Shakespeare: The Poet in His World.* New York: Columbia University Press, 1978.

Brown, Cedric C., ed. *Patronage, Politics, and Literary Tradition in England, 1558–1658.* Detroit, Mich.: Wayne State University Press, 1993.

Buxton, John. *Elizabethan Taste.* London: Harvester, 1963.

Cheyfitz, Eric. *The Poetics of Imperialism: Translation and Colonization from* The Tempest *to* Tarzan. New York: Oxford University Press, 1991.

Cowan, Alexander. *Urban Europe, 1500–1700.* New York: Oxford University Press, 1998.

Dolan, John P., ed. *The Essential Erasmus.* New York: New American Library, 1964.

Finucci, Valeria, and Regina Schwartz, eds. *Desire in the Renaissance: Psychoanalysis and Literature.* Princeton, N.J.: Princeton University Press, 1994.

Fumerton, Patricia, and Simon Hunt, eds. *Renaissance Culture and the Everyday.* Philadelphia: University of Pennsylvania Press, 1999.

Greenblatt, Stephen J. *Learning to Curse: Essays in Early Modern Culture.* New York: Routledge, 1990.

Halliday, F. E. *Shakespeare in His Age.* South Brunswick, N.J.: Yoseloff, 1965.

Harrison, G. B., ed. *The Elizabethan Journals: Being a Record of Those Things Most Talked of During the Years 1591–1597.* Abridged ed. 2 vols. New York: Doubleday Anchor, 1965.

Harrison, William. *The Description of England: The Classic Contemporary [1577] Account of Tudor Social Life.* Edited by Georges Edelen.

Washington, D.C.: Folger Shakespeare Library, 1968. 2d ed., New York: Dover, 1994.

Huizinga, Johan. *Erasmus and the Age of Reformation.* New York: Harper and Row, 1957.

Jardine, Lisa. *Reading Shakespeare Historically.* London: Routledge, 1996.

———. *Worldly Goods: A New History of the Renaissance.* London: Macmillan, 1996.

Jeanneret, Michel. *A Feast of Words: Banquets and Table Talk in the Renaissance.* Translated by Jeremy Whiteley and Emma Hughes. Chicago: University of Chicago Press, 1991.

Kernan, Alvin. *Shakespeare, the King's Playwright: Theater in the Stuart Court, 1603–1613.* New Haven: Yale University Press, 1995.

Lockyer, Roger. *Tudor and Stuart Britain.* London: Longmans, 1964.

Rose, Mary Beth, ed. *Renaissance Drama as Cultural History: Essays from Renaissance Drama, 1977–1987.* Evanston, Ill.: Northwestern University Press, 1990.

Schmidgall, Gary. *Shakespeare and the Courtly Aesthetic.* Berkeley: University of California Press, 1981.

Tillyard, E. M. W. *The Elizabethan World Picture.* London: Chatto and Windus, 1943. Reprint, Harmondsworth: Penguin, 1963.

Willey, Basil. *The Seventeenth Century Background: Studies in the Thought of the Age in Relation to Poetry and Religion.* New York: Columbia University Press, 1933. Reprint, New York: Doubleday, 1955.

Wilson, F. P. *The Plague in Shakespeare's London.* 2d ed. Oxford: Oxford University Press, 1963.

Wilson, John Dover. *Life in Shakespeare's England: A Book of Elizabethan Prose.* 2d ed. Cambridge: Cambridge University Press, 1913. Reprint, Harmondsworth: Penguin, 1944.

Zimmerman, Susan, and Ronald F. E. Weissman, eds. *Urban Life in the Renaissance.* Newark: University of Delaware Press, 1989.

Dramatic Development

Cohen, Walter. *Drama of a Nation: Public Theater in Renaissance England and Spain.* Ithaca, N.Y.: Cornell University Press, 1985.

Dessen, Alan C. *Shakespeare and the Late Moral Plays.* Lincoln: University of Nebraska Press, 1986.

Fraser, Russell A., and Norman Rabkin, eds. *Drama of the English Renaissance.* 2 vols. Upper Saddle River, N.J.: Prentice Hall, 1976.

Happé, Peter, ed. *Tudor Interludes.* Harmondsworth: Penguin, 1972.

Laroque, François. *Shakespeare's Festive World: Elizabethan Seasonal Entertainment and the Professional Stage.* Translated by Janet Lloyd. Cambridge: Cambridge University Press, 1991.

Norland, Howard B. *Drama in Early Tudor Britain, 1485–1558.* Lincoln: University of Nebraska Press, 1995.

Theater and Stage

Doran, Madeleine. *Endeavors of Art: A Study of Form in Elizabethan Drama.* Milwaukee: University of Wisconsin Press, 1954.

Gurr, Andrew. *Playgoing in Shakespeare's London.* Cambridge: Cambridge University Press, 1987.

————. *The Shakespearian Stage, 1574–1642.* 3d ed. Cambridge: Cambridge University Press, 1992.

Harrison, G. B. *Elizabethan Plays and Players.* Ann Arbor: University of Michigan Press, 1956.

Holmes, Martin. *Shakespeare and His Players.* New York: Scribners, 1972.

Ingram, William. *The Business of Playing: The Beginnings of the Adult Professional Theater in Elizabethan London.* Ithaca, N.Y.: Cornell University Press, 1992.

Lamb, Charles. *The Complete Works and Letters.* New York: Modern Library, 1935.

Marcus, Leah S. *Unediting the Renaissance: Shakespeare, Marlowe, Milton.* London: Routledge, 1996.

Orgel, Stephen. *The Authentic Shakespeare and Other Problems of the Early Modern Stage.* New York: Routledge, 2002.

Salgado, Gamini. *Eyewitnesses of Shakespeare: First Hand Accounts of Performances, 1590–1890.* New York: Barnes and Noble, 1975.

Stern, Tijffany. *Rehearsal from Shakespeare to Sheridan.* Oxford: Clarendon Press, 2000.

Thomson, Peter. *Shakespeare's Professional Career.* Cambridge: Cambridge University Press, 1992.

Weimann, Robert. *Shakespeare and the Popular Tradition in the Theater: Studies in the Social Dimension of Dramatic Form and Function.* Edited by Robert Schwartz. Baltimore: Johns Hopkins University Press, 1978.

Yachnin, Paul. *Stage-Wrights: Shakespeare, Jonson, Middleton, and the Making of Theatrical Value.* Philadelphia: University of Pennsylvania Press, 1997.

Biography

Halliday, F. E. *The Life of Shakespeare.* Rev. ed. London, Duckworth, 1964.

Honigmann, F. A. J. *Shakespeare: The "Lost Years."* 2d ed. Manchester: Manchester University Press, 1998.

Schoenbaum, Samuel. *Shakespeare's Lives.* New ed. Oxford: Clarendon Press, 1991.

———. *William Shakespeare: A Compact Documentary Life.* Oxford: Oxford University Press, 1977.

General

Bergeron, David M., and Geraldo U. de Sousa. *Shakespeare: A Study and Research Guide.* 3d ed. Lawrence: University of Kansas Press, 1995.

Berryman, John. *Berryman's Shakespeare.* Edited by John Haffenden. Preface by Robert Giroux. New York: Farrar, Straus and Giroux, 1999.

Bradbey, Anne, ed. *Shakespearian Criticism, 1919–35.* London: Oxford University Press, 1936.

Colie, Rosalie L. *Shakespeare's Living Art.* Princeton, N.J.: Princeton University Press, 1974.

Dean, Leonard F., ed. *Shakespeare: Modern Essays in Criticism.* Rev. ed. New York: Oxford University Press, 1967.

Grene, David. *The Actor in History: Studies in Shakespearean Stage Poetry.* University Park: Pennsylvania State University Press, 1988.

Goddard, Harold C. *The Meaning of Shakespeare*. 2 vols. Chicago: University of Chicago Press, 1951.

Kaufmann, Ralph J. *Elizabethan Drama: Modern Essays in Criticism*. New York: Oxford University Press, 1961.

McDonald, Russ. *The Bedford Companion to Shakespeare: An Introduction with Documents*. Boston: Bedford, 1996.

Raffel, Burton. *How to Read a Poem*. New York: Meridian, 1984.

Ricks, Christopher, ed. *English Drama to 1710*. Rev. ed. Harmondsworth: Sphere, 1987.

Siegel, Paul N., ed. *His Infinite Variety: Major Shakespearean Criticism Since Johnson*. Philadelphia: Lippincott, 1964.

Sweeting, Elizabeth J. *Early Tudor Criticism: Linguistic and Literary*. Oxford: Blackwell, 1940.

Van Doren, Mark. *Shakespeare*. New York: Holt, 1939.

Weiss, Theodore. *The Breath of Clowns and Kings: Shakespeare's Early Comedies and Histories*. New York: Atheneum, 1971.

Wells, Stanley, ed. *The Cambridge Companion to Shakespeare Studies*. Cambridge: Cambridge University Press, 1986.

FINDING LIST

Repeated unfamiliar words and meanings, alphabetically arranged, with act, scene, and footnote number of first occurrence, in the spelling (form) of that first occurrence.

abhorred	1.2.292	*butler*	Char. 3
abide	1.2.362	*by and by*	2.1.8
advance	1.2.390	*case*	1.1.45
affection	1.2.429	*chapped*	1.1.65
air	1.2.382	*charge*	1.2.435
allay	1.2.3	*charm* (noun)	1.2.250
amazement	1.2.12	*cheek*	1.2.6
apes	2.2.10	*common*	2.1.2
art	1.2.1	*credit* (verb)	1.2.103
attend	1.2.70	*delicate*	1.2.290
bate (verb)	1.2.269	*delivered*	2.1.27
bestow	4.1.38	*demanded*	1.2.151
blow (verb)	3.1.51	*dew*	1.2.246
bow	2.1.77	*dispersed*	1.2.239
brave	1.2.7	*distractions*	3.3.69
brine	1.2.233	*else*	1.2.37

serious	2.1.141	trial	1.2.442
service	1.2.267	tricks	1.2.232
several	3.1.37	used	1.2.353
sinews	3.1.21	very	1.2.26
slave	1.2.288	warrant	1.1.48
something	1.2.396	wench	1.2.152
(adverb)		wherefore	1.2.149
springs (noun)	1.2.343	wink'st	2.1.139
stomach	1.2.177	worthy	1.2.267
supplant	3.2.25	wrack	1.2.25
time	2.1.229		